Everyone's Book of Veteran and Vintage Cars

Everyone's Book of

Veteran and Vintage Cars

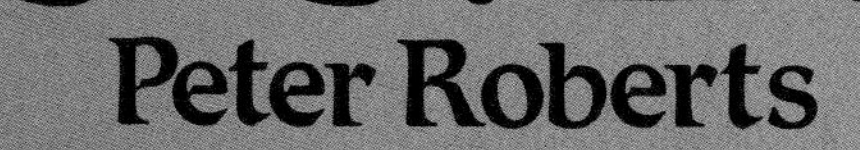

This edition published exclusively for W H Smith

Published by
The Hamlyn Publishing Group Limited
London · New York · Sydney · Toronto
Astronaut House, Feltham, Middlesex, England

ISBN 0 600 37886 1

Printed in Italy

The author and publishers would like to offer their sincere thanks to the following persons and organizations for their valuable help in compiling this book, both in the matter of editorial research and illustrations:

Adam Opel AG; Alfa Romeo SpA; American Motors Corporation; Automobiles Citroën; Automobiles Peugeot SA; Mr. Michael Banfield; Mr. Cecil Bendall; British Leyland UK Limited; Chrysler Corporation; Daimler-Benz AG; Fiat SpA; Ford Motor Company Limited; General Motors Corporation; Lips Autotron, Holland; Mercedes-Benz (UK) Limited; Musée de l'Automobile Française; Norddeutches Auto Motorrad Museum; Régie Renault; Mr. Peter Richley; Rolls-Royce Motors Limited; Sotheby's; Stratford-upon-Avon Motor Museum; Vauxhall Motors Limited; Victoria and Albert Museum, Bethnal Green, London.

Photographic acknowledgments
Neill Bruce: page 67. Mary Evans Picture Library: page 6 bottom. Harrah's, Reno, Nevada: page 49 top. Nicky Wright: pages 69, 76, 77 bottom. (The photograph on page 77 bottom is also by permission of the Auburn-Cord-Duesenberg Museum.)
All other photographs are from the Peter Roberts Collection

Front cover: Bugatti 51A, 1932 (Tony Stone Associates)
Back cover: Mercedes Benz SSK 38/250, 1927 (Colour Library International)
Endpapers: Veteran and Vintage Car Rally (Peter Roberts)
Title spread: Mercedes Sportswagen S, 1927 (Peter Roberts)
Contents spread: Opel Doppel Phaeton 1908 (Peter Roberts)

Contents

The Impossible Dream

'When we see'd that Captain Dick was agoing to turn on steam, we jumped up, as many as could, maybe seven or eight of us. 'Twas a stiffish hill going up to Camborne Beacon, but she went off like a little bird. . . . She was going faster than I could walk, and went up the hill about half a mile further, when they turned her, and came back again to the shop.'

So said a passenger of Britain's first self-propelled road conveyance as he marvelled at its short journey around the Cornish lanes on Christmas Eve 1801.

Richard Trevithick, mining engineer and builder of steam road and rail vehicles, and designer of high-pressure steam engines, made several other journeys in this lumbering carriage before he left it in an inn stable one evening, forgetting to extinguish its boiler's fire. The coach was burned to a cinder – and Trevithick was thrown out of the inn.

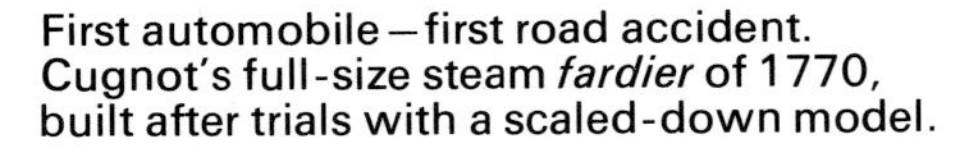

First automobile – first road accident. Cugnot's full-size steam *fardier* of 1770, built after trials with a scaled-down model.

His second attempt at a road-carriage was considerably more successful. Trevithick, having studied the works of steam pioneer Watt, and of French engineer Cugnot who had made and driven his steam artillery gun-tractor some 32 years earlier, designed and constructed the first-ever self-propelled road vehicle. Built in 1803, the Cornish engineer's vehicle was a massive piece of machinery with a boiler at the rear of a high-placed coach body. Surprisingly reliable, it could transport nine passengers at around 9 mph. Trevithick wrestled the high coach up and down London's Oxford Street, lurching over potholes and terrifying horses and pedestrians alike. Unfortunately he found no sponsors, sold the great engine to a mill owner, and died in penury. However, it was an historically appropriate moment for development of a new form of mobility. England at the end of the 18th century was using nearly three million horses to power its transport. Long-distance travel was virtually nil; only the nobility or the military ventured to move from their own locality. It was just as it had been since the Middle Ages. Yet industry was beginning to move away from the cottage-craft labour of past centuries. World trade was flourishing, bringing imports to the coastal regions of Britain where, as often as not, they stayed, unless a

Right: Hancock's steam carriage 'Enterprise' of 1883.

Second-generation steam power. This steam phaeton built by the partnership of Comte de Dion and boiler-maker Georges Bouton was one of a number of successful vehicles.

navigable river was at hand. In 1769, the same year as Cugnot had shown his first steam *fardier* to the French authorities, James Watt had patented his stationary steam engine, giving birth to the cotton and engineering industries. By 1800 the industrial revolution was in full spate. Fast cheap transport was urgently needed.

After the Napoleonic wars commerce leapt ahead in Europe even more rapidly. In Britain Telford and MacAdam opened the way for increased road travel by improving construction and surfacing methods, allowing a network of horse-drawn vehicles to link up most of the major towns in Britain. When the world's first railway, running from Stockton to Darlington in the North of England, was opened in 1825, steam pioneers endeavoured to produce some sort of public passenger road vehicle that could compete with the railways. During the 1820s and 1830s several were built and used successfully. Goldsworthy Gurney's steam carriages made regular runs from Cheltenham to Gloucester at an average speed of 12 mph, a shade faster than the highly efficient horse-drawn mail coaches of the day, and more flexible than the infant railways. Another steam-coach service of nine vehicles plied regularly through London during the third decade of the 18th century. These were the steam diligences of Marlborough-born Walter Hancock, the first of which, a toast-rack type of charabanc called *Infant*, scurried about London with a dozen passengers in the 1830s. In 1833 two more, the *Autopsy* and *Enterprise*, were built – the latter being closed-bodied like an omnibus – and were used on city runs. Hancock's steam coaches carried 12,000 passengers through the London region within five months covering over 4,000 miles without major disaster.

These steam-coach companies developed the world's first successful mechanical road transport systems, but England's lead in automotive travel was lost forever when strong horse-coach interests caused heavy tolls to be levied on turnpike roads and country boundaries, singling out steam carriages for the most punitive charges. Further aggravated by politically backed competition from the railways, now spreading their network rapidly over the United Kingdom, the first essay into mechanical road transport finally ground to a halt. Grass began to grow over the winding roads of Britain once more. . . .

Steam power in really practicable form was next seen in France some 40 years later (although many engineers had built their own experimental 'road locomotives' during the middle years of the 19th century) in the steam carriage of Amédée Bollée, scion of a respected bell-founding family. His large twin-engined steamer, a high-balustraded vehicle with something of the look of a mobile grandstand, astonished Parisian strollers one autumn day in 1875 as it arrived chuffing down the Champs Elysées after rumbling the 230 km (143 miles) from its stable at Le Mans.

But if the internal combustion engine is to be considered the first genuine power unit of the first automobile as we know it today, then German engineers Benz and Daimler must share the credit for founding the industry. Although Belgian Etienne Lenoir had built a gas-engine *circa* 1858 and installed it in a cart-type vehicle the following year, his ignition-at-atmospheric-pressure unit was extremely inefficient. The Lenoir engine, however, encouraged a young German clerk, Nikolaus Otto, to adapt it for use in situations where steam power was impracticable. He formed a company, Gasmotoren-Fabrik Deutz, with engineer Eugen Langen, and employed a 38-year-old factory manager then living in Karlsruhe, one Gottlieb Daimler, who became intensely interested in developing Otto's engine using petroleum distillates as fuel.

The career of Karl Benz had brought him into contact with the Otto four-cycle engine at the time of a family crisis, causing Benz to switch from his attempt to produce tin-working machinery to engine design. He made a small two-stroke unit, then in 1884 he cranked-up his first four-stroke unit with electric ignition . . . and the heart of the world's first motor carriage began beating in the small tool shed in a Mannheim suburb.

This set of Edwardian cigarette cards shows man's early attempts at mechanical transport.

Birth of the Motor Age

German engineer Karl Benz advertised his new 'Patent Motor Car' in the technical press for the first time in 1888.

The reports of his first demonstration had been varied. One stated that his motor carriage would be 'as little promising as the use of steam engines for road transport'; others were more favourably impressed. Said a Munich newspaper: 'Seldom if ever have passers-by in the streets of our city seen a more startling sight than on Saturday afternoon when a one-horse chaise came . . . down Herzog Wilhelmstrasse at a good clip without any horse, a gentleman sitting under a Surrey top, riding on three wheels – one in front and two behind – speeding on his way to the centre of town. The amazement of everyone who saw him was such that they seemed unable to grasp what they had before their eyes, and the astonishment was general. . . .' A fulsome if somewhat non-technical report of the first sighting of Benz car No. 1.

Gottlieb Daimler's 'single-track' machine of 1885. The tiny 0·5-litre (½-hp) single-cylinder engine turned at about 700 rpm.

There was more in this vein in the report and, for 2,000 Marks, the price was considered modest. Benz waited hopefully for the first orders. There were none. The still unproved vehicle needed promotional elevation.

Benz's two sons, Eugen aged 15 and Richard 13, decided to prove the little one-horsepower three-wheeler on a long-distance run. They persuaded their mother Bertha to join them in their enterprise.

At 5 am one Sunday morning in August 1888, while their father was still asleep, the three set out on what was later to be recognized as the first significant cross-country journey ever made by an automobile. Today the short trip from Mannheim on the Rhine to Pforzheim at the edge of the Schwartzwald, a distance of about 80 km (50 miles) would take perhaps 45 autobahn minutes in a modern Mercedes-Benz. In August 1888, however, it was an historic marathon for the first Benz.

First they drove from Mannheim to the main road township of Weinheim, negotiating small gradients that would be totally unnoticeable today, but which to these first-timers were hazards that forced all but the

Above: Karl Benz, living and working just a few miles from Daimler, also made his first motor vehicle in 1885. This three-wheeler, Patent DRP 37435 of 29 January 1886 was driven by a one-cylinder four-stroke unit. Its top speed was 15 km/h (about 9 mph).

Left: An artist's impression of early motoring – with a competitive flavour. The marques defy recognition, but the one on the right looks Benz-based.

driver to get out and push. At Wiesloch they made their first stop, for water; then an *apoteke* (apothecary) was found who could supply petroleum fuel, a fluid which in those days was used mainly as a cleaning agent. With Eugen at the steering lever, Frau Benz sitting next to him on the narrow bench and young Richard in the backwards-facing occasional seat, the frail car was driven on towards Bauschlott, a village only some 5 km (3 miles) from their destination. Here a shoemaker supplied them with a block of leather to replace a worn-through brake pad, and yet more water. Skirting a mountain road near the end of the journey they arrived in Pforzheim in late evening. Too weary to pay the intended courtesy call on relations, the travellers put up for the night at the modest Gasthaus Zur Post. A crowd soon gathered in the dusk, appraising the bizarre little carriage – one gloomy fellow announced prophetically that he would forthwith go home and kill off his dray horse as its day was over. Benz Senior was contacted by telegraph the following day. Local dignitaries congratulated the pioneer motorists – Frau Benz for her fortitude and the boys for their ingenuity in making a number of repairs: replacing slipping chains, mending an electrical fault in the ignition, clearing a blocked fuel line.

Karl Benz wrote years later in his memoirs that after his first fright at the dangers of such a journey, pride in his family's initiative was his prime emotion. And at least one useful modification, a lower gear for hills, was directly attributable to their unique motor journey.

The first of Benz's motor carriages was built in 1885, after he had broken with his company to produce gas-engined cars of his own. He used the engine he had designed a few years earlier, 'a dwarf in weight but a titan in power' as he described the one-horse unit. His definition of gas was – 'gas vapourized from a liquid by means of an apparatus carried on the vehicle', as distinct from several early engines that had operated on coal or 'town' gas, which of course needed no 'apparatus' (carburettor) to vapourize it.

The structure of the car was based on bicycle-building principles: lightweight, with large slender-spoked wheels. Only three road wheels were used as Benz had not yet learned the trick of steering through two front wheels – that was to come later with his four-wheeled Viktoria of 1894.

Benz produced this Viktoria (so named for his victory over the intricacies of the geometry of four-wheel steering) in 1893–4. This entirely new car was fitted with a larger engine than earlier models – a 2·9-litre unit that could develop 3 hp.

This light carriage was Daimler's 'birthday present' to his wife in 1886. The shafts for the horse had been removed and a 1·1-litre one-cylinder vertical engine installed. Drive was to the rear wheels and the unit was water-cooled.

This 1897 Daimler has a V-twin engine – Daimler's development of his first vertical single-cylinder unit – giving just 4 hp. The tonneau body has a central rear entrance and can seat five. It is seen here on the historic Commemoration Run from London to Brighton.

The first Opel, based on a design by locksmith Friedrich Lutzmann of Dessau. A Benz-influenced 4-hp, this Opel Patent Motor Wagen had to be detuned down to a 12-mph maximum speed to stay within the law.

A tiny single-cylinder motor, turning at some 250 rpm, powered the light vehicle from just behind the bench seat, aided by a heavy horizontal flywheel. Karl Benz had devised his own ignition system (even fabricating his own spark plugs) and had developed a simple evaporation carburettor. A camshaft operated valves and ignition, a flat belt-drive went to a countershaft which housed a differential, and side-chains took the drive onwards to the rear road wheels. Benz tested the car privately in late 1885, and on public roads on 3 July 1886. He was greatly encouraged when a top speed of 15 km/h (9 mph) was achieved.

At this time another dedicated engineer living and working less than 100 km (60 miles) away from Benz was developing a mechanically driven road vehicle along very similar lines. However, Gottlieb Daimler's prime aim was to build an engine capable of propelling anything from a riverboat to an airship. The fact that he first made a road vehicle was almost incidental.

However, Daimler's two-wheeled 'single track' machine, a rudimentary motorcycle, housed his first engine purely as a handy test-bench. This was also a single-cylinder unit, but its working speed was considerably higher than the Benz engine, giving about ½ hp at 700 rpm.

Then, in April 1886, Frau Daimler's 'birthday' present appeared. Daimler had ordered a light carriage to be made and delivered secretly to his workshop in Cannstatt, explaining his clandestine attitude by saying that it was to be a surprise for his wife. Removing the shafts and adding centre-pivot steering gear, he mounted his engine on rubber blocks to damp vibration (an innovation that was re-introduced many years later), installed fan cooling, a friction clutch, a two-speed gearbox and a simple rear-wheel differential system that allowed road-wheel cornering compensation. The 52-year-old engineer then tried out his horseless carriage in the works yard and found to his delight that he could conduct it at speeds up to 18 km/h (11 mph). Then his assistant and old friend, Willi Maybach (who perhaps should be given more credit for early Daimler designs than history allows), drove this, the world's first four-wheel car, out through the gardens of the Esslingen Works. For good or ill, the motor age had dawned.

While Daimler went on to develop his engine, producing by 1889 a narrow-V twin-cylinder unit which was used under licence in several European countries as soon as they woke up to the fact that the automobile age was upon them, his main interest shifted towards powering various other forms of transport. He built and used the world's first motorboat on the nearby Neckar River. He installed his engine in an early airship, a tram car, rail transport vehicles – everything that could be motorized. But road vehicles eventually claimed his soaring imagination, leading by the end of the century to a line of increasingly efficient automobiles and eventually to the one that was to be a dramatic watershed in the infant automotive industry – the Mercedes.

BRUTAL, MAIS ÇA MARCHE!

The company of Panhard et Levassor had long been in the business of making woodworking machinery. They naturally showed interest in such events as the 1889 World Fair in Paris, in which a number of steam and petroleum engines were shown. One stand featured the compact V-twin unit – now developing twice its original power – offered under licence by Gottlieb Daimler, who also displayed a new motor car, his 'Stahlradwagen' or Steelwheeler.

The Steelwheeler was a radical departure from the adaptions that Daimler had previously made to carriages of established design, in which he installed his engines. This was a vehicle built with little reference to traditional methods (and, in fact, showed some of the cycle influence that had been evident in the earliest Benz car in its lightweight concept). It had four forward speeds, the new V-twin engine and geometrically correct two-wheel front steering. It aroused almost no interest at all at the Paris Show. However, Daimler's engines captured the imagination of a small section of the public, largely due to his bright idea of using one to power the electricity supply to 30 incandescent lamps at the stand, calculated to catch the eye of passers-by.

Luckily for Daimler – and for France – designer-engineer Emile Levassor's affianced lady, Mme Louise Sarazin, a widow whose husband had been a friend and colleague of the Würtemburger car-builder, had earlier acquired a licence to manufacture and sell the Daimler engine. An astute businesswoman, she had agreed to pay for the rights only as soon as the engines had earned a profit. Emile Levassor must have been impressed. He married Mme Sarazin the following year and his company commenced building Daimler engines.

By February 1890 Panhard et Levassor had made their first car, a mid-engined dog-cart affair that was soon changed to a more stable layout. P & L No. 2 was the historic vehicle that the motor industry recognizes as

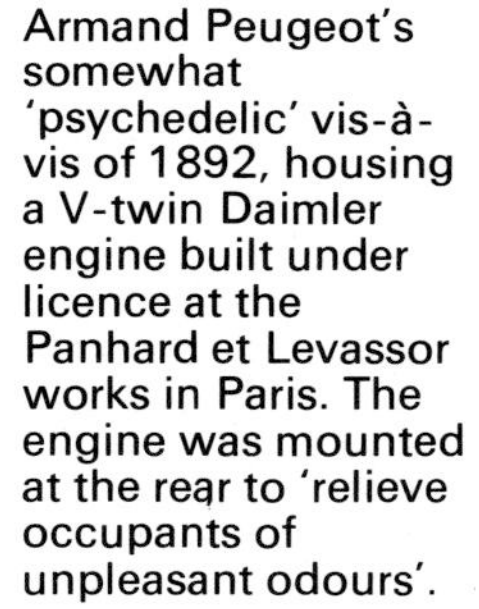

Armand Peugeot's somewhat 'psychedelic' vis-à-vis of 1892, housing a V-twin Daimler engine built under licence at the Panhard et Levassor works in Paris. The engine was mounted at the rear to 'relieve occupants of unpleasant odours'.

Left: Panhard et Levassor, 1895. By this time Emile Levassor had developed an engine of his own design, the vertical-twin Phoenix, which was beginning to be fitted into Panhard cars in place of the Daimler-designed unit.

the first automobile with what soon became the normal distribution of mechanics and drive train – front engine, drive through clutch and gearbox to the rear wheels – and with seating and driving positions much as they have remained for almost a century.

The engines for sale at Panhard attracted the eager interest of Armand, son of Emile Peugeot, who had established a prestigious company manufacturing cycles and hardware. The company had built its fortunes on an earlier revival in demand for their steel rods to support the latest fashion in crinolines. When the fashion faded, the metal rods were modified into spokes for high-wheeled cycles. A Peugeot quadricycle using a Daimler petrol engine was soon built at 'Les Fils de Peugeot Frères' factory at Valentigney. Young Peugeot, who had studied production methods in several English factories, moved rapidly into automobile-making, producing between 1891 and 1894 no less than 64 *quadricycles à 4 places* with the Daimler V-twin engine, cone clutch and four-speed *boîtes des vitesses* (gearboxes). Top speed on the level was a creditable 18 km/h (11 mph).

Although these primordial Peugeots were among the first internal-combustion engined vehicles, they were by no means the only self-propelled road vehicles on French roads at the time. Steam power pre-dated petroleum fuel, and French engineers, since the days of Cugnot in the 18th century, had been fascinated by mechanical transport. Blacksmith's son Léon Serpollet had long been a steam pioneer, as had former bell-founder Amédée Bollée; Comte de Dion had earlier joined boiler-making expert Georges Bouton to produce a range of steam buses and tractors (the latter used for towing road carriages), breaks and tricars, and were on the brink of making a successful high-speed petrol engine.

That France should be the venue of this rapid resurgence of road transport after almost half a century of the railroad's dominance as the prime – almost the only – method of long-distance travel is not surprising. Industrial supremacy lay with Great Britain and France during the ageing 19th century. Germany had been a loose union of small states until

The underside of a De Dion, *c.* 1897. The alfresco transmission seen here must have operated in a mud-bath during wet weather.

Below: An Italian poster of 1899 showing a cyclist ('cads on castors', as many were known) offering his salutations to Signora. Prinetti & Stucchi may have had a good line in advertisements (and motor tricycles), but sadly their car-manufacturing company lasted only a brief two years.

Bottom: The Benz Velo of 1894, successor to the Viktoria, was Karl's first quantity-produced model aimed at a 'popular' market. In its basic form it cost a modest 2,000 Marks. Its maximum speed was about 20 km/h (12 mph).

comparatively recently; the United States was still tinkering in the backyard with its naive high-wheel buggies; Italy, recently unified, had little immediate commercial potential. However, Britain, birthplace of the railways and of organized road transport, wanted little to do with the 'nasty explosion machines' brought in from Germany and France. Landowners were horse-owners (or railway investors) and nobody was going to disturb their established order of life.

In France, on the other hand, Napoleon had built magnificent roads in long straight lines down the length and breadth of the country and the French were determined to use them. Vehicles of a dozen designs proliferated.

Young '*automobilistes*' very soon began to use their vehicles as sporting chariots, and many were the unofficial and unrecorded races held in the latter years of the last century.

History tells us that the first competitive event in motoring was held on 22 July 1894, and this trial of reliability, run from the Porte Maillot in Paris to the centre of Rouen, some 126 km (78 miles) northwest, has passed into legend over the years. The somewhat chaotic contest designed by newspaper editor Pierre Gifford to encourage the building of more reliable motor vehicles by offering prizes for the machine that was 'the least dangerous, most easily handled and of low running costs', developed into a race as soon as the first *concourants* had trundled their wagons around the first corner. The event is well documented and the stories of the hazards of the route are legion. Enough here to state that 21 vehicles of assorted shapes and principles arrived at the start-line, including one or two whose driving systems would have baffled an Einstein. Some were steam-driven, first cousins to a railroad locomotive, needing both a *conducteur* (driver) and a *chauffeur* (stoker) to shovel in a constant supply of coke. In fact the first arrival at Rouen, a De Dion Bouton steamer, was disqualified on this point. The more conventional were powered by the petrol engine of Herr Daimler, who had actually come to Paris – by train – to view the event. Stops for rest and lunch were included, and as crews fell out of the contest with their vehicles *hors de combat* they were picked up by following competitors and given a lift to Rouen.

A Gardner-Serpollet steamer of the turn of the century. Steam was popular at this time and competed strongly with petrol as a propellant, although it had several handicaps such as delayed starting. A steam vehicle built by Frenchman Léon Serpollet captured the world speed record as early as 1902 – at an astonishing 120·1 km/h (about 74 mph).

It almost goes without saying that a Panhard and a Peugeot, the two most sophisticated marques of France, shared the victor's prize. The first 13 places were taken by petrol-driven cars, while almost half the steam entrants dropped out. This Alice-in-Wonderland sporting event had lasting results; it established the internal combustion engine as the most convenient and reliable power for personal road transport. Steam vehicles were made and used over the following years, as were electric cars, but although their advantages were several, the petrol engine, arguably the least efficient, won prime place in the development of the automobile.

MEANWHILE . . . BACK IN MICHIGAN

The United States at the end of the last century was teeming with young and vigorous innovators. In the fields of electrics and chemistry, agriculture and mining, America was bulging with ideas, and the will to make them concrete.

Eager mechanics were blacksmithing together simple gas buggies in a thousand backyards. Many of the spidery results actually ran – and a handful of them clattered out of the woodshed into history. One such was a quadricycle made by a farmer's boy from Wayne County, Michigan, young Henry Ford.

Henry had been fascinated by mechanics since he was 12 years old, had made a miniature steam engine at 15, and now in the winter of 1893, in the coal shed at the bottom of his garden in Bagley Avenue, Detroit, he was cobbling up a primitive gasoline engine out of a piece of old metal piping, supplying a spark from the electrical house-wiring, and getting his young wife, Clara, to drip-feed gasoline into the end of the pipe. Not much of an engine for 1893 perhaps when in Europe half-a-dozen makes used the roads, but it was one of the first in the U.S.A. whose history, until recently, had been more concerned with national survival than mechanical transportation.

Three years later, in 1896, Henry Ford put his popping little motor, now considerably improved, into a primitive vehicle. Soapbox construction was supported by bicycle suspension and running gear. His featherweight auto boasted no brakes, no reverse gear, no steering wheel. The car's two-cylinder engine had a choice of two forward speeds by belt-and-pulley adjustment. On test day it was found to be too wide to go through the shed door, so Henry impatiently grabbed an axe and hacked a way out for his first automobile in true auto-pioneer tradition!

Built in a garden workshop in Detroit, Michigan, in 1896, Henry Ford's first soapbox car was driven by this little two-cylinder unit. Its top speed of 20 mph surprised even its maker.

Ford's employer, Thomas Edison, was equally enthusiastic. 'You have it,' the great inventor told Henry. 'Keep at it!' Ford did, and made a few false starts, one of which was to form the Henry Ford Company which ploughed into financial trouble and was taken over by engineer Henry Leland who changed the name of the company to Cadillac in 1903, with historic results. Henry Ford finally found backers and formed a new company in 1903. Twelve shareholders put up $28,000. The lucky gamblers sold their stock back to the company some time later; two lawyers who had put up $5,000 each, cashed in a total of $25 million!

The ubiquitous Model T, first seen in 1908, touched off the automobile habit in the U.S.A., which soon spread worldwide. By 1913 when Ford opened a new sophisticated mass-production works in Michigan, his empire was supreme in the automotive world.

Not that Ford was the first in the quantity-production field, or even the first in assembly-line car-making. There were earlier pioneers, and others whose contribution was to be significant.

The Duryea brothers are acknowledged as the first to build a saleable car in the U.S.A.; their Benz-based buggy was born in 1893 and publicly demonstrated in 1896 at Springfield, Massachusetts. Elwood Haynes had built a car in 1894, another single-cylinder buggy-type vehicle, and had, a couple of years later, joined the Apperson brothers to produce a series of two- and four-seater cars by 1898. By 1899 there were about 60 companies in the United States that were engaged in manufacturing cars, more than in any single country in Europe, although their total production was smaller than that of Europe.

Ransom Eli Olds, originally a steam buff, built a number of electric cars in the late 1890s, before moving on to constructing petrol-driven cars at Lansing, Michigan, forming his company in 1896 and designing his famed Curved-Dash Runabout in 1901. The Curved-Dash was in fact the first-ever car to be quantity-produced. Olds, whose plans for building a factory for the exclusive purpose of making cars caused him to be thought something of a 'cockeyed optimist' as the current song went, managed to find a few others of similar sanguinity, and drummed up approximately $500,000. His enterprise flourished, perhaps partly because his maxim was to build vehicles 'simple, economical and durable, *with as little confusion to the operator as possible*'. But his greatest piece of luck occurred on one fine afternoon in 1901 when his factory burned to the ground. This 'blessed disaster', as it was later called, forced the company into single-model manufacturing. The one-and-only demonstration model of the Curved-Dash had been rescued from the conflagration, and was put into production.

The new Oldsmobile production line was several years ahead of the standard practice for those hammer-and-anvil days. It was a genuine, if simple, progressive assembly line. The cars were rolled on wheeled platforms from one work-group to another, each attaching (mainly bought-in) parts from conveniently placed storage boxes. The U.S.-based *Automobile Magazine* was wide-eyed in its report. 'The motors (engines) were passed step by step, down the assembling bench, towards the testing department which is in the next room, a new piece being added at every move with clocklike regularity.' These little 7-hp horizontal single-cylinder engines

The ubiquitous T. Ford's 'Tin Lizzie' of 1908 sparked off a worldwide change in mass transport, from horse to horsepower.

A popular American model. This tiller-steered Curved-Dash Oldsmobile one-cylinder has a 7-hp horizontal motor and simple controls and would bowl along at a steady 15 mph, its engine going 'one chug per telegraph pole'.

with their 'one chug per telegraph pole' were destined to power some 12,000 Curved-Dash Oldsmobiles between 1901 and 1905, an enormous figure for a time when few citizens of the U.S.A. – or anywhere else in the western world for that matter – had ever *seen* an automobile, let alone ridden in one. And when one considers the state of the inter-city 'highways' of the American continent at that time, where roads generally ran out of paving just beyond the city limits to degenerate into cart tracks for the rest of any journey, it may be imagined that motorists travelled only when it was absolutely unavoidable in winter.

However, the state of the roads – contemporary wits averred that it was simpler to go round the U.S.A. than to try to drive across it – did little to retard the healthy proliferation of automotive companies. Many were formed, made their brave essays and, as often as not, foundered on the reefs of technological or financial inadequacies. Some, the ones that hit the right market level or had something better to offer, went on to fame and fortune. Names like Cadillac (formed 1903), Packard (1899), Buick (1903), Winton (1897), Pierce (1901), various steam cars such as White and Stanley, and rival electrics of sundry makes shared a major portion of the U.S. market in the halcyon days around the dawn of the new century. Half a dozen years earlier when a few friends – Leland, Ford, Olds, Buick, and one or two others – had met for an occasional beer in a downtown Detroit bar, they could not have guessed that the Michigan town would become the world's greatest automobile manufacturing crucible, and that their pipe-dream empires would become vast and powerful organizations that would change the face of the civilized world.

RESISTANCE TO CHANGE

While American newspapers blazoned headlines that extolled the new method of transportation as early as 1889, just four short years after Daimler and Benz had built their first motor vehicles, Britain, bastion of the equestrian world, showed every sign that she wanted things to stay that way on her green and leisurely country roads.

'A Marvellous Motor', 'A New Propelling Power that Has Come out of Poetic Germany', 'Horse Traction Falling into Disuse', expressed American sentiments and a fulsome press praised the automobile for its potential in solving the serious pollution problems caused by the horse . . . a very different attitude from those in authority in the last days of Victorian England. . . . In Britain it is the spring of the year 1896. A perspiring man in a stovepipe hat walks down a residential roadway. He carries a small red flag over his shoulder. Sixty yards behind him, a horseless carriage wheels slowly along, carrying its driver and passenger at a full 4 mph. Any increase in speed would incur a five-shilling fine, and English bobbies were all too eager to use their new stop watches.

Cars in Britain were still classed as road tractors under a decree of some 30 years earlier, when the success of steam road vehicles had posed a threat to the prosperity of the railways and were legislated off the roads. A man to walk in front, said the law, no vehicle to exceed 4 mph. 'It is enacted by the Queen's most excellent Majesty' the 1865 Act opened . . . and went on to define, with a touch of *perpetuum mobile*, a road vehicle as 'every locomotive propelled by its own power and containing within itself the machinery for its own propulsion . . .' and continued '. . . that at least three people shall be employed to conduct such a locomotive . . .' and closed with the edict that these vehicles should consume their own smoke. It was this Act that brought the first system of steam buses and coaches in England – a network that had operated efficiently and regularly since the 1830s – to a final grinding, hissing halt. Incidentally Her Most Excellent Majesty had once sworn never to enter 'one of these nasty smoky motor carriages'.

Below left: Early superstructure styling closely followed horse-and-carriage tradition. Phaetons, vis-à-vis, victorias, sociables and landaulettes merely changed their method of propulsion from horse to horsepower. This is an 1897 Benz dogcart.

Below: Programme for a pioneer motor show: Richmond, 1899. The first indoor show held in Britain was the Stanley Cycle Show in 1895, where five motor cars were exhibited.

Overleaf: This English-made (Channel Islands) Benz of 1899 is a dos-à-dos (back-to-back seating) with a $4\frac{1}{2}$-hp engine horizontal single-cylinder water-cooled engine and two-speed transmission.

CO-83

Old interests and prejudices, then, were the major reasons for Britain's lagging entry into the automotive world. While France was holding motor races to encourage use of the new transport and Germany was making cars in commercial numbers, Britain was trundling along behind the man with the flag until 14 November 1896. Before this date there had been 'daredevils' who had purchased cars from overseas, and there were several enterprising British engineers who had actually built cars. Among the latter was Frederick Lanchester, who made his first prototype in 1895, with a philosophy (if not design) similar to Benz – i.e. ignoring, as far as practicable, traditional coachbuilding methods and stationary engine practice. Until 1914 Lanchester engines were horizontally mounted midships. Each piston had its own crankshaft and flywheel, the ride was silky-smooth and, at a time when a driver normally had to pressure-feed oil to essential moving parts regularly and often by hand-plunger, the Lanchester was automatically lubricated. Few machines could match its advanced technology.

The first production Lanchester emerged from the Birmingham factory in 1900, although a prototype car of advanced design had been running since 1896. This is a two-cylinder 10-hp of 1903, with some elaborate lighting equipment.

But apart from this single early British example, the infant motor industry was slow to grow. Gottlieb Daimler had made a contract with Englishman Frederick Sims, who also had a business in Hamburg and who was planning to import Daimlers to England. This brave move was taken three full years before the shackles were struck off by the Act of Parliament of November 1896 – the 'Emancipation Act' allowed cars to travel at speeds of up to 14 mph. The British motor age was creeping into view.

The Act released the energies of a number of engineers who had hitherto been mainly concerned with the cycle trade that had long flourished in England's Midlands (which had become a world centre for the machine that had first brought real mobility to the common man). Now, the De Dions, Peugeots, and Benz Velos imported from Europe would have competition.

Even before the 1896 Act there had, of course, been rumblings in high places. A machine like the motor car, with its ramifications as visible to the Englishman as to 'liberated' Europeans, could not be ignored. By the time Edward, Prince of Wales, then still waiting in the wings for his crown, had been given a few rides by the clever John Scott Montagu and others, and had himself dropped a few hints within his influential circle, motoring was bound to arrive at the shores of Albion.

Right: A Benz sociable at speed. Its date of manufacture is 1895, its velocity a breezy 29 km/h (18 mph).

Veteran Years

Motor manufacture in both Continental Europe and the U.S.A. began to expand – to explode – in 1899. It was more than evident that the automobile had an assured future, and even Britain had held its first annual Motor Show in 1898. One only had to go to a horse sale to find that horses were going for the price of penny buns.

It had taken about ten years since the first days of Benz and Daimler to persuade a select band of pioneer owners who were wealthy enough to be able to purchase and maintain the expensive machine, that the autocar, *voiture*, or *motorwagen* was the smart item to buy. Peugeot sales, for instance, had been climbing rapidly: 178 Phaetons, Quads, Victorias and Vis-à-Vis between 1894 and 1897, plus a breakway into commercial vehicles, and then an overwhelming 1,200 units between 1898 and 1902. During this time Peugeot's designs had evolved from carriage-style runabouts with large bicycle-type wire wheels and underseat Daimler units with a top speed of 15 km/h (9 mph) to smart front-engined tonneau or spider cars with twin horizontally opposed cylinders giving up to 8 hp and a sportive 30 km/h (19 mph).

Now when Madame went for a morning ride round the Paris Bois, it was her chauffeur who conducted her vehicle down the fashionable avenues, not a bewigged coachman. Some women even drove themselves, meeting male

American steam was alive and fighting for supremacy in the early 20th century. Locomobile bought the steam rights from the famous Stanley brothers, and produced a line of somewhat crude tiller-steered models that consumed rivers of water and had poor lubrication. This 1901 model has been well preserved, however, and is fully operational today.

Wind-in-the-Willows scorchers on their own ground, although most Edwardian ladies sent their grooms to one of the new motor schools. 'In the hunting season I ride, in fine weather I enjoy driving,' said one English lady. Those lady drivers who insisted, long before the self-starter took the hard labour out of starting-up in 1912, on risking the hazards of the open road received much advice from the press. Male writers would warn the delicate sex that 'driving needs a strong determined character, trained by the constant exercise of the body and mind, and absolute lack of nerves . . . which must generally be lacking to most women whose lives are not passed in a rough hand-to-hand tussle with life . . .' and much notice they took of *his* sage words. Lady drivers were told that 'one needs to prepare for local motoring by removing one's rings . . . as one finds that the constant vibration from the steering wheel as it passes over undulating road surfaces will rattle their stones loose in no time. . . .' Another chose to recommend that a small hand mirror should be carried by any lady who may venture out in her motor alone, for rearward viewing.

By 1902 automobiles were becoming relatively sophisticated. This 10-hp Benz had a twin-cylinder power unit of 2710 cc and a healthy top speed of 45 km/h (28 mph). The blind spot in design seems to have been weather protection, although large plate windscreens were available for some models.

A journalist of some repute and early female motorist warned that some of the courtesies of the road may confuse even the best of chauffeuses, and that 'one should not leave the engine running when outside a house. It may annoy the inmates. . . . Allow cyclists a wide berth. . . . Do not sound your siren in town. . . . Remember that mail vans have the right of way. . . .' and advises that half-a-crown given to the groom on a visit to a friend will always be welcome. With the state of the horse business in Edwardian days one could understand.

While the new sport of motoring was taking over from tennis and trout fishing for the upper crust of the old world, much was happening of a more serious nature in the mills of industry.

The crucible that Detroit was to become was already being heated. After the first generation of autobuggies had captured the interest of the eccentric and the bold, the wheels of finance and commerce and new technology began to turn, to found and to consolidate a fast-growing industry. The bluff ex-cavalryman Theodore Roosevelt was in America's driving seat; Carnegie was pouring out rivers of white-hot steel; immigrants were crowding into the country, jostling for the privilege of working; and oilfields were beginning to be recognized as reservoirs of the world's commerce.

When machine-tool designer Henry Leland took over the ailing Henry Ford Company in 1903, his aim, like Henry Royce, was to produce a car that he would be able to call 'The Standard of the World'. He renamed the

firm the Cadillac Automobile Company, and first went into production with a car that looked superficially like Ford's first model made by his new concern the Ford Motor Company, just down the road in Michigan's budding auto-city.

Leland and Cadillac became bywords for quality. His maxim that parts should be made so accurately that they could be interchanged without difficulty – this in an age when parts were ground-and-filed individually to fit one specific 'mate' – was proved in a bold demonstration a few years later: he dismantled three Cadillac cars, scrambled the parts together, had the cars rebuilt on the spot, and sent them immediately on a 500-mile test run.

Leland had competitors. One, James Ward Packard, had entered the automotive field a little earlier than Leland, in 1899. He had bought a Cleveland-made Winton and decided he could do better. Packard commenced making cars in 1899 and was reasonably successful. However, the marque received its greatest impetus when former railroad man Henry Joy went to the 1901 New York Automobile Show to buy a steam car, got showered with hot water for his trouble, chanced to see a Packard being started on a single gentle swing of the handle – and dashed straight to Warren, Ohio, to put his money in the firm. Joy's influence turned a minor company into one of the great American manufacturers.

Such were the razor-edges of fate that brought the industry to its peak some years later. Not that the field was open to benign fortune all that often. There were no less than 2,900 first-generation automakers in the U.S.A. in the early days of the century. The vast majority were to go to the wall before the First World War, and all but a handful disappeared by the time the Wall Street crash of 1929 had burnt out.

Ford was moving in the direction of a popular car in 1900–5 period but, as yet, Henry had not set down the design of his legendary 'flivver', the Model T. His backers had persuaded him to build a big six-cylinder luxury car although he said he 'didn't like a car with more plugs than a cow's teats' and, indeed, the Model K never really caught on with the hard-working folk of North America.

Above: The Packard 30 of 1907, the Pierce Arrow of 1909, and the six-cylinder Peerless series were prestige cars from America's classic trinity, with prices to match.

Top: American gunsmith Henry Leland renamed the ailing Henry Ford Company the Cadillac Automobile Company, creating a new high standard of quality in U.S. automotive production. The first Cadillacs of 1903 housed single-cylinder 7-hp underfloor engines.

Henry Ford's lasting success was ensured with his formation of the Ford Motor Company. His Model N of 1906, seen here, is a direct forerunner of the enormously popular Model T, launched in 1908. The Ford N, a best-seller of its day, was a lightweight four-cylinder machine which cost just $500.

A simple man with a simple philosophy, Ford had long wanted to produce a simple car. By 1906 he had put the Model N on the market (the car that was later developed into the T), the first four-cylinder car in the country that sold (at $500) for less than the reliable but dated single-pot Cadillac, which remained in production until 1908.

Another entry was a Scottish emigré, David Buick, then living in Flint. His trade as a plumber had introduced him to machine-making and he worked with single-minded devotion on his own internal combustion engine. By 1902 he had produced a fine two-cylinder valve-in-head (overhead-valve) unit. Money ran out and wagon-making tycoon William Crapo Durant (a name to conjure with in American auto history) took over the Buick factory. Later the company became the foundation stone of General Motors, gargantua of the vast American automotive industry. Buick, himself, left the company early to vanish from the scene, but his name still decorates the cars that roll off the lines at Flint, Michigan.

By 1905 the days of experiment had moved into a period of sophisticated commercial production. Sewing-machine companies, bicycle firms and other light engineering organizations had turned to automobile manufacturing – often with the somewhat reluctant agreement of shareholders – but this was a time, the beginning of a new century, when everything was starting to happen – wireless communications, cinema, the new popular press, heavier-than-air flight – and new industries were not to be denied, either in emergent America or Edwardian England.

It was also happening in Wilhelmine, Germany. Old Adam Opel had, way back in 1863, offered his own sewing machines to the good people of Russelsheim near Frankfurt. Opel's wife and five sons took over the business when he died in 1895 but not before Karl, Wilhelm, Heinrich, Fritz and Ludwig had persuaded him to turn to producing bicycles, the rage of the time.

The five Opel boys made their first horseless carriage in 1899 with the help of Friedrich Lutzmann, one-time court blacksmith to the Duke of Anhalt. The car was Benz-based with a 4-hp water-cooled single-cylinder rear engine, belt-and-pulley to countershaft and final drive by chain – a fairly standard system for the day, and surprisingly reliable.

The car could make about 20 km/h (12 mph), quite fast enough for the roads of those days (just try sitting in a rear-engined one-lunger of the turn of the century as its chuffs along at a smart canter; there is so little forward protection that it seems like double the speed and completely out of control), and the little cars sold well, as did the Opel-Darracqs a couple of years later. When the Opels completely made the car a Russelsheim concurrent with gaining a number of race victories, Opel started the climb that was to make it a large force in Germany, accounting for nearly 40 per cent of that country's automobile production at its peak.

Scottish emigré David Dunbar Buick formed his company around his well-designed power unit, a two-cylinder overhead-valve engine. This is a 1906 Buick, the 22-hp Model F.

A few hundred kilometres southeast, an infant motor industry was also developing near the Tatra Mountains in Nesselsdorf, Moravia (later to become part of Czechoslovakia) where a young engineer was beginning to show an unusually perceptive grasp of automotive principles and practice. Hans Ledwinka came from a traditional background. Nephew of a locksmith, he had showed mechanical aptitudes from childhood. His first post was at the Waggonfabrik Ignaz Schustala, a firm making rolling stock for the railroads of central Europe. As it happened the company was just about to produce its first car (and in so doing carved a pioneer's niche for itself in the industry, for this was three years before the end of the century) and was saved from disaster by young Ledwinka, who restructured a flawed transmission design.

By the end of 1899 the Nesseldorf 'Präsident' prototype had been shown and the company had produced ten copies of the Benz-based flat-twin carriage. After a few years in Vienna making steam cars, Ledwinka returned to his old firm to design the highly successful 30-hp 3·3-litre Type S in 1906. The Nesselsdorf company, one of the founders of the European auto industry, is a long-forgotten name, as is its mainstay, Hans Ledwinka, who as the pioneer of such advances as four-wheel brakes, air-cooling, rear engine and backbone chassis, deserves a more marked place in the history of motor design.

Overleaf: The former sewing-machine company of Adam Opel marketed its first car in 1899 in collaboration with engineer Lutzmann, then with the French Darracq firm. By 1902 Opel had launched its own complete car, a 10/12-hp twin-cylinder shaft-driven vehicle with mechanically operated valves and steering-column gear-shift.

This pot-bellied 1904 Spyker featured in *Genevieve*, the classic film that sparked the renaissance of the Veteran car movement. A four-cylinder engine turning at about 1500 rpm develops 18 hp. Its top speed is around 60 km/h (40 mph).

While still in central Europe mention should be made of another far-sighted engineer of the time, the man, in fact, who had designed that prototype Nesselsdorf with its faulty transmission, Dr. Edmund Rumpler. It was one of the Bohemian engineer's few errors of design. The world knew him during the First World War as a brilliant designer of aeroplanes. The Taube, with its swept-back single wing, was one of the most effective German air weapons of the war.

Perhaps Rumpler's most astonishing feat was the design of the car known as the *Tropfenwagen* (Teardrop car) first seen in 1921. It was like Benz's first car, built with a dedicated disregard of established practice.

Powered by a 2,580-cc rear-mounted six-cylinder engine with gearbox built in unit, the design was completely new with the cylinders in arrowhead layout in three banks of two. The body, shaped like a tadpole on a strict diet, was aerodynamic at a time when most road vehicles were matchbox-shaped. The central driving position and flat-plate wings were clearly influenced by Rumpler's aircraft experience, and the drag co-efficient must have been lower than that of several present-day designs. The Benz company took up Rumpler's design and produced their *Tropfenrennwagen* (Racing Teardrop), reflections of which could be seen in Auto Union racing cars of some ten years later.

LOUIS OF FRANCE

The noise of hammering down at the bottom of the garden nearly drove the neighbours of the Renault family to the nearest magistrate during the spring months of 1898. Their son Louis, a cadaverous 21 year old, had bought a De Dion tricycle, rejigged it to accommodate four wheels, made a gearbox to replace its belt-system, and put in a drive-shaft to a differential on the back axle assembly. The gearbox had three forward speeds, one of which was Renault's own 'direct drive', carrying the power straight through from the engine via the main shaft to the rear wheels through bevel gears. Smooth, modestly efficient and very new, Renault's little car caught the eye of *Maître* Viot, a friend of Renault's father, who asked for a ride. On Christmas Eve, 1898, Louis drove lawyer Viot up the steep hill to the Butte Montmartre in Paris. Viot slapped down 40 gold Louis on a café table and Renault's first car was sold. Other friends clamoured for a trip in the light vehicle, and within hours no less than 12 orders were placed.

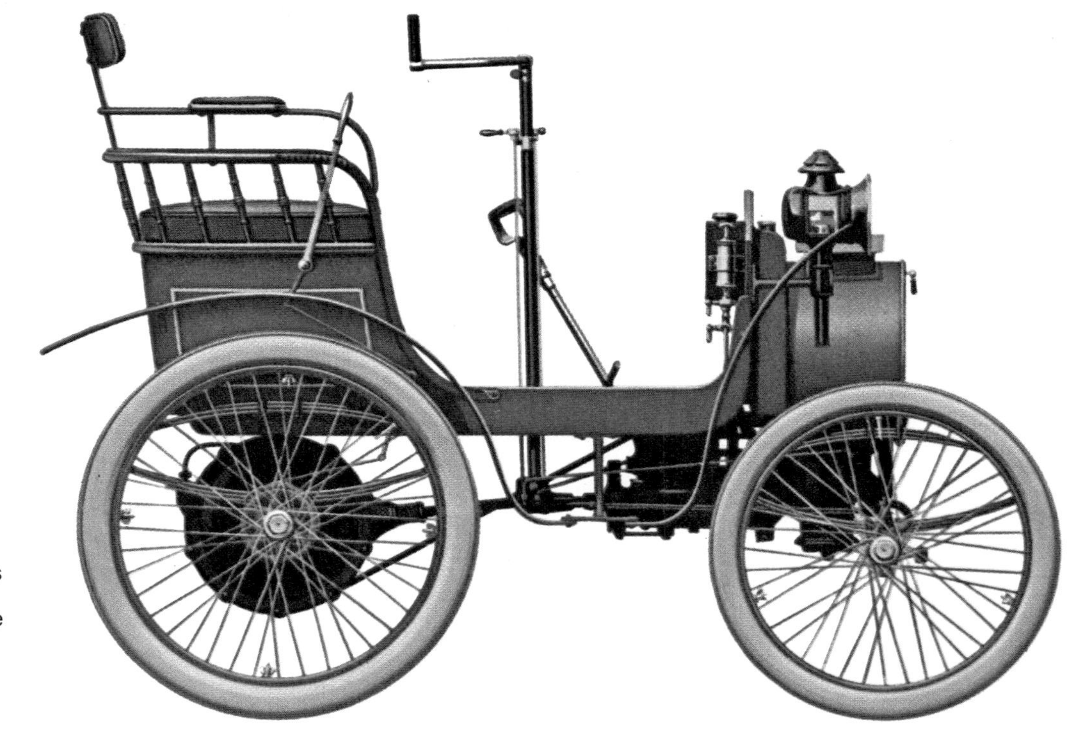

Right: An 1899 Renault. With this little 1-hp single-cylinder voiturette Louis Renault built a motor-manufacturing empire.

A four-cylinder 12-hp Clement, produced in France in 1903, speeds along an English country road.

Thus was the Renault company founded. It grew into so great an empire that in later years it was to become part of the national wealth of France.

At first, Renault Frères (Louis, Marcel, Fernand: Company assets Fr. 60,000) used 3·5-hp water-cooled De Dion engines – almost every manufacturer of the time used either Daimler's V-twin or the adaptable little De Dion unit. Then, in 1902, they decided that four-cylinder units were necessary, bought a batch of engines made by Viet, and won the Paris-Madrid race that year. They could cope with the resultant flood of orders only by enlarging their Billancourt, Paris, factory. In addition Louis' direct-drive patent was being taken up by other motor-makers, all of whom were paying him a handsome royalty.

Although Germany had been the cradle of the automobile, it was nurtured in France, which by 1903 was the leading motor manufacturing nation, with some 30,000 road vehicles made that year. Renault Frères wanted a larger share in this bonanza and so, in addition to building larger cars, began to manufacture taxis. They were destined to become part of history.

The 1100-cc two-cylinder '*Deux Patte*' taxis that were first seen on the Paris *pavé* one day in 1905 (the local Hackney Carriage Company had placed a giant order with Renault) brought about a new and efficient way of cross-city travel, with metered fares and far greater speed and comfort than the old one-horse *fiacres*. They were an immediate success, spreading to other large European cities, even to diehard London. Well before the First World War London had several thousands plying its wood-block streets – so many that some condemned London taxi-riding as unpatriotic!

Garage service, 1905. Bearded Monsieur and his *petite amie* leave the repair shop in their car, to the doffed caps of the staff!

Renault's great moment in the annals of French history came in 1916 when the French front line was threatened and Paris itself was in imminent danger. The German First Army under General von Kluck had crossed the Marne and had thrown allied troops into confusion. Fresh French troops were desperately needed at a point near Nateuille-Haudoin, and the railroad could handle only about half the number required. The French General Clergie ordered that all taxis in Paris should be requisitioned, loaded with five men each and driven as fast as possible to the front line. Six hundred taxis made two such trips, undoubtedly saving the French capital. The drivers were, by the way, paid double fare and were also awarded a *supplement* (tip) of 27 per cent. It says much for the almost-indestructible Renault taxi that only four broke down en route.

During those early years of the century, France's *grandes marques* were the low-slung CGV, the aristocratic De Dietrich, the rotund Delauney-Belleville (introduced in 1905) and others, and the best-sellers were Peugeout, Panhard and De Dion Mors were the fastest, and had performed some almost unbelievable feats, including a well-authenticated average in the 1902 Paris-Vienna race of no less than 114 km/h (71 mph) over a 100-km (62·5-mile) stretch. During the run it overtook an express train as though it was a piece of roadside furniture.

ENGLAND AWAKE!

Men, like former gas-engine expert F. W. Lanchester, had been experimenting with a high-speed petrol engine for ten years before the market was ready for their products. But with the Emancipation Act of 1896

Right: A De Dion-Bouton, 1903. The small but efficient De Dion engines were used in over 140 different makes of car around this period. Author Peter Roberts is the driver here.

Rural England was changing under the wheels of the automobile, too. Much advice was given through the press about the hazards of motor driving, but dust was the major problem.

when the footman with the red flag was pensioned off and speeds in excess of walking pace grudgingly permitted, Fred Lanchester and brother George took their new advanced 5-hp car on its first trial run. Within five years, Albert Edward was Britain's new monarch and, although many cynics predicted that he 'wouldn't be half the king his mother was', he was a motoring enthusiast, and things augered well for the bright new age of the automobile.

There were naturally one or two clouds on the new motoring scene: the police, in particular, were well under the thumb of local magistrates, who were themselves invariably in close league with the local landowners. Sometimes, indeed, they were the very same people. Most rode to hounds; few loved the motor car. Nevertheless, the new sport of 'automobilism' was enthusiastically taken up by the small côterie of less conventional people who could afford powered transport. Most purchases were made as part of the stern pursuit of pleasure, an essential ingredient of Edwardian social life. Wrote one scribe of the day: 'Both for shooting and fishing, rapidity of transport will do wonders . . . the new mode of locomotion will make river, loch and forest accessible from the same centre . . . if there are duck pits and snipe marshes at certain (separate) places on the property. With two good motor cars you can take four or five guns and loaders; you can visit all these places in a day.' A sentiment almost as sadly Edwardian as the pathos unconsciously expressed in 'the motor is left on the road at the spot nearest the stream, and should you decide in favour of another sport, or return home . . . you can rejoin your wife . . . or possibly go on to "bridge" or "ping-pong".' A dedicated pursuit of divertissement indeed.

But back to the factory. In 1903 Herbert Austin was still designing cars for Wolseley but was in trouble for his prejudice in favour of the horizontal engine when other Wolseley technicians were recommending a change to vertical cylinders. Herbert left a little later in some dudgeon to set up his own company at a disused factory at Longbridge near Birmingham in the English Midlands. There, in 1906, he produced a chain-driven 25/30-hp car. It had a vertical engine.

Another man of technical maturity, Northerner Henry Royce, had bought a French Decauville car in 1902, sniffed disparagingly at its blacksmith mechanics, and made a considerably better one in his Manchester workshop. As a cranemaker Royce was a success; as a motor manufacturer he was a perfectionist, and when his little 10-hp two-cylinder car was first shown to the public, their praise knew no bounds. This self-made man, who had started his working life aged 12 as a scarecrow for a local farmer, had made the first of a line that would be a byword for that which is peerless, and the name of which would become part of the language. When 'Pa' Royce met aristocrat Charles Rolls, they formed a team in 1904 that proved unbeatable. Silence and reliability had been the watchwords from the beginning, and the latter was proved when an original

Above: English family transport. An Alldays (made by the Alldays and Onions Pneumatic Company of Birmingham) swing-seat tonneau of 1905. It combined elegance with a 1·6 twin-cylinder unit and shaft drive.

Left: 'Pa' Royce made his first car in 1904. By 1906, just two years later, Rolls-Royce had launched the car which made their legendary reputation, the 40/50-hp Silver Ghost.

owner returned his 1905 1·8-litre 10-hp car to the works in 1923 asking if the company would like to accept it as a museum-piece as he hadn't the heart to sell it. It had covered well over 100,000 miles of Scottish hills and was still in perfect order. Amusingly, once this offer became generally known, so many long-term owners offered their cars back to the company in gratitude for lifetime reliability that Rolls-Royce had, reluctantly, to turn them down!

Other manufacturers of significance were emerging in the first decade. The Rover Company of Coventry had been makers of penny-farthing cycles as early as 1878, later inventing something they called the safety-cycle, a rear-driven two-wheeler with same-size wheels front and rear – the cycle we use today, no less. In 1902 a motorcycle appeared and two years later a little 8-hp car was offered. Rover cars were to win many early sporting events, and later, after a period of small-car making, went on to acquire a secure niche in the quality market, and to pioneer gas-turbine motors.

Daimler – the British variety – had been well established by 1904, when a thorough re-organization took place. Daimler cars had been sold in England since 1895 when they were imported from Germany by arrangement with H. J. Lawson's dubious Daimler Motor Syndicate. In 1897 the first British-made Daimlers were seen, built on Panhard lines, with two-cylinder engines and larger-diameter rear wheels. At this time a Phaeton cost £368 complete

Daimler – British variety. The earliest to be built at the Coventry factory were two-cylinder cars made to a design licensed by Panhard. This 38-hp seven-seater may still be seen motoring along in full vigour today.

(about £8,000 today), a sum that would exclude all but the most wealthy purchasers.

When the Prince of Wales expressed a wish to experience a journey in a motor car on public roads for the first time, Daimler were quick to produce an example for his use. The royal client had already ridden in a Serpollet steamer on one of his watering visits to Bad Homburg in 1893, and had been taken out for a spin in an earlier Daimler. In 1899 he had also been driven around by the Hon. John Scott-Montagu, father of the present Lord Montagu of motoring fame, and had had the time of his princely life. There had been a couple of ladies present (weren't there always, ever since pretty little Nellie Clifden in 1861) and they had been driven around the open roads of Hampshire, achieving a frightening (and illegal) 40 mph, a traumatic experience for newcomers to motoring on the roads – and the suspensions of those days – to say nothing of the altitude of the passengers on the towering vehicle. The ladies had to hang on to their hats, which prompted the Prince to forecast a change in headgear fashion due to the increasing popularity of the motor car, a prediction in the right direction but well short of the truth.

The Prince bought three Daimler cars in 1900 and later granted the Royal warrant to the company as suppliers to the crown. His son, George V, carried on the Daimler tradition, as did *his* son George VI, who used nearly a thousand Daimler cars at his coronation. The first years of the 1900s saw

For the impecunious in 1904, a Rexette forecar. It has three wheels, a single-cylinder engine, cycle-type construction – and a passenger seat 'nearest the accident'. It was made in Birmingham and Coventry.

Daimler making larger and more powerful cars as the head-of-state image took over following the royal patronage.

Down the social scale a little were a number of solid British companies, each capturing its own market. Vauxhall Ironworks Limited, previous makers of marine engines, had moved up-country to Luton with their little three-cylinder 6-hp and were by 1905 producing a selection of vehicles, including one incredible motorized 'Hansom' cab with the driver sitting high at the rear in a position guaranteed to decapitate him at the first low bridge. Other companies included marques such as Alldays, Sunbeam (a former tinplate-and-japanning company), Rexette (a little tandem vehicle that looked like an invalid motorcycle but was popular at the lower end of the market), Riley (another motorcycle-influenced lightweight), Crossley (a car built around a well-known engine), Napier (a society carriage with a turn of performance and made by the first British company to market a six-cylinder car successfully), Thornycroft (large and solid with a steam-engine background), Star, Horbick, Albion, Swift (a one-lunger until 1904) and so on. By the end of 1905 the total number of manufacturers in Great Britain alone approached 300. And when in 1906 the figures of British road users was published, the country was found to be positively teeming with 23,192 cars.

RIVIERA DEBUT

A motoring debut that occurred during the first year of the century has not yet been mentioned. It was an event that shocked current manufacturers, that astonished the cognoscenti, that superannuated every other car at a stroke, and that overnight defined the modern automobile as we know it: the appearance of the first Mercedes in the spring of 1901.

Gottlieb Daimler had died in 1900, but his partner, Maybach, continued to produce improved designs from the Cannstatt works. By March 1901 he was ready to show his latest model to the general public, a successor to the Daimler Phoenix that had been entered in the previous year's sportive week in Nice on the French Riviera. The Niçe Week's programme for 1901 was a sort of general junket up and down local hills and races along the coast roads to nearby towns. It was also the social event of the season, the wily Niçoises and Monagasques even then knowing how to fill their hotel rooms through the doldrum months.

During the stiff hill climb up to La Turbie, the village that towers above Monte Carlo, Daimler driver Willi Bauer had overturned his car the previous year with fatal results. Emil Jellinek, the Daimler agent for the South of France, was disturbed. With this accident plus the fact that the Panhard cars were eating into his sales, he needed a car that would provide spectacular competition. He asked Wilhelm Maybach to produce a model with a much lower centre of gravity and a turn of real speed. Maybach obliged in good time for Nice Week, 1901.

The German cars' 'social' debut (they had been seen briefly on a race-track two months earlier) was dramatic. In the face of top European competition, the new and untried cars, identity masked by the pseudonym 'Mercedes', the name of agent Jellinek's 11-year-old daughter, were the

The Canstatt Daimler of 1899, 'prototype' grandfather of the Mercedes. Its short wheelbase and high centre of gravity proved dangerous, a fact which led directly to the lower, faster Mercedes of 1901. This car was built as a racing vehicle for the famous driver Count Zborowski.

centre of interest. Three examples were sent to Nice that March, to be driven by established racing drivers from Germany. The mysterious Mercedes won almost everything in sight, and later sat on the promenade bedecked with bouquets of exotic flowers for all to admire. Said a journal of the day about the speed event from Nice to Salon, near Avignon, and back: 'The car ran the full course – which is so hilly that high speeds thereon are regarded as impossible – of 500 km (279·45 miles), at an average speed of 58·94 km/h (36·63 mph), passing through no fewer than thirty villages in that distance wherein speed must be reduced to 12 km/h (7½ mph). . . .' Try that in a modern car sometimes, avoiding the *autoroute*, and the difficulty of keeping up a modest average of 60 km/h on those winding roads through the scrub forests will be appreciated.

The first of the Mercedes line. Its appearance and successes in 1901 at the Nice Spring Sporting Week rendered all other motor cars of the time antiquated overnight. Its 35-hp 5·9-litre engine, its transmission and its frame and suspension marked perhaps the most dramatic milestone of design and performance in motoring history.

Jellinek, an excitable little pince-nez-and-panama Leipziger, was overjoyed. He wanted to know how many could be made in the year, was promised 35 and presented his cheque for the entire series. He then sold them to his eager friends on the Côte d'Azur at the usual margins.

The Mercedes' victories during Nice Week caused French journalists to bemoan the fact that their country's Mors and Panhards, Darracqs,

Right: The Mercedes-Simplex car of 1902. Direct successor to the 35-hp Mercedes that confounded its rivals, this 40-hp 60-km/h (40-mph) luxury tourer was even lighter and faster than its forebear.

Renaults and Gobron-Brilliés were eclipsed by the German cars' vivid performances. Paul Meyan, doyen of the sporting press, quoted Jellinek as saying, 'That car is nothing beside what you'll see next year.' Was he bluffing, asked Meyan? Emil Jellinek was not, and further shocks were in store for the automotive world when the second generation of the line appeared in 1902, the 40-hp Mercedes, first of an ever-growing series.

The first 35-hp Mercedes, white and low and completely different from any previous model of any known marque, introduced, in one clean sweep, many of the fundamentals of what we think of as today's standard automobile.

Firstly, common to almost all cars of the time was a chassis of armoured wood. The Mercedes had a pressed-steel chassis – stronger, less whippy, more durable, lighter. That would have been enough to make it a milestone. It was also much lower built than others and its wheels were all the same size; most designs then still used larger-diameter rear wheels. The standard quadrant (through which the gear lever was moved in a single plane back and forth in an arc) was replaced by the gate-change, which in principle is still used in modern cars. The Mercedes had four forward speeds. Compared with the clatter of its contemporaries, the Mercedes 5·9-litre engine

The Michelin Tyre Company's advertisements were international even way back at the turn of the century – this is a Russian poster of the period.

whispered. Mechanically operated inlet valves were used, when others were satisfied with the less efficient atmospheric system using the descending pistons to 'suck' the inlet valves open. Water-cooling was achieved by honeycomb radiator with integral water-tank, when cooling was usually accomplished by a long pipe bent laboriously back and forth and covered with small fins to disseminate heat. The car had the new Mercedes patent helical-spring clutch. It had pneumatic tyres. Its raked steering wheel allowed better control. A transmission brake and internal-expanding brakes on the rear wheel put its stopping power ahead of most of the field.

In short, the new car from Cannstatt was cause for much gnashing of teeth in an industry which, nothing if not opportunist, promptly got down to the task of copying as much of the new Mercedes as it possibly could. Many rival models that appeared over the next few years show an extraordinary similarity to the 35-hp Mercedes of 1901. Although produced primarily as a touring vehicle, the Mercedes was soon taken up by the more sporting *autocarists* and was soon to become a strong contender as a racing vehicle.

There followed a great range of Mercedes models from Cannstatt, many of which sold in France, now that the weighty Teutonic name of Daimler was missing from the product.

A brief conversation at the 1902 Paris Exposition tells us of how rapidly motoring had advanced in the previous two years or so, in this case, in the matter of acceptable cruising speeds. Designer Willi Maybach was chatting to King Leopold of Belgium, a keen driver who owned a 40-hp Mercedes. 'Unless I can touch 130 km (about 80 mph) per hour,' said the king, 'the car is no use to me.' Maybach replied with a typically technical piece of information that he could manufacture a car capable of more than that – of any speed. 'But,' he said, 'speed does not increase in the same ratio as engine power; the latter has to be quadrupled if the speed is to be doubled.'

And that briefly was the problem that exercised most automotive engineering minds over the next ten years.

The Long Summer

The Edwardian period in Britain had shifted into top gear by 1906; in France the automobile's *Belle Epoque* was showering its delights upon the motorist. The U.S.A., still energetically digging its resources out of its vast landmass, was beginning to realize that, after the British Empire faded, it would be its own turn in the halls of power.

Motoring was no longer a novelty, although its role, at least in Europe, as an essential part of day-to-day working life, had not yet been established.

However, internal-combustion vehicles had taken over much of the work of traditional transport, both commercial and personal. Since 1903 all British motor cars had been registered (numbered like convicts and labelled like hackneys, said some) and the shape of the car had long since settled down to a conventional layout – one knew, more or less, where everything was, underneath. With the exceptions of eccentrics like Lanchester (still mid-engined in 1908), the London-made N.E.C. with its underfloor horizontal engine and a few others, the superstructures were all very similar in profile – a squared-up front with spade mudguards to scoop up the flying mud, the long shafts of brake and gear lever on the outside of the cab, a hefty raked steering column topped by a wooden wheel positioned to massage the driver's waistcoat.

Nostalgia for the generation before last – some badges bearing the evocative names of long-gone marques.

Right: The Rover 20-hp of 1907. Although conventional in shape and engineering, this model achieved its pinnacle of fame by winning the Tourist Trophy Race at the Isle of Man that year.

High seats of leather button-upholstery – even the cheaper models were thus lavishly equipped – were almost without exception exposed to the elements front and sides. Drivers were still assumed to be hardened sportsmen in these alfresco days, and front doors were still not considered necessary. Rear passenger accommodation for the larger car (designed for the ladies of course) was luxurious, often with *Roi-des-Belges* seats – a hip-wrapping double couch reputedly designed by King Leopold after his mistress had expressed a desire for armchair travelling comfort. Wheels, still wooden-spoked, and small passenger side doors (or a central rear door) completed the conventional automobile of mid-Edwardian production.

A four-cylinder front-engine, driven by propeller shaft rather than chains, was normal from about 1907, led by the new 40/50-hp Rolls-Royce Silver Ghost and, although leather cone clutches were still common, multiple discs were on the way in. The one- or two-cylinder engine was being dropped and

Overleaf: Leather-upholstery period piece – an Opel 'Doktorwagen' of 1909. It provided solid workmanship and convenience for the professional user.

ROVER
ROV
4
DUNLOP CORD
DUNLOP CORD

a number of sizes were offered. High-tension ignition was almost universal and mechanical force-feed lubrication was advancing.

As prices went up, so did the cape-cart hoods – even though it would take two skilled assistants to erect the braced soft-top into place. When folded back for fine weather they looked more like emergency parachutes than rain-tops.

If the standard car of around 1908 looked exactly like any other in profile, it certainly was not true of the front view. Here, now that the rush to design a Mercedes look-alike radiator was over, artistic engineers had really gone to town. Popular was the Delaunay-Belleville rotunda, a pot-bellied radiator that still held a hint of the marque's steam forebears; its cachet – *très snob* – had brought in followers such as Maudsley (Coventry-built), the Dutch Spyker, the 46-hp Britannia, the Porthos from Billancourt near the Renault works, and a number of others. Some automobiles sported pear-shaped radiators, diamond shapes, squashed parallelograms, Parthenon shapes (Rolls-Royce), coal-scuttle shapes (Renault) and shapes that cried out for an aspidistra in the filler cap. And all with their unprotected honeycomb cooling cells boldly facing the flinty road.

European steam and electric cars were by now sadly only for steam and electric enthusiasts.

Eminent writer Aldous Huxley used 1 October 1908 in his best seller of the 1920s as beginning '*The Year of Our Ford*', deifying Henry of that name in his socio-science-fiction epic, *Brave New World*. A lot of other people closer to old Henry might also have given him a fairly elevated rating about this time, too, for October 1908 was certainly a turning point of the world's personal mobility problems.

Though millions of words have been written about it, songs composed about it, films created for it, the Model T, Ford's greatest contribution to his generation for good or ill, must be mentioned here. For the Model Ts – all

Rich man's toy? This one was certainly a rich child's toy. A limousine by Georges Carette, it dates from 1911 and was first sold in Nuremburg.

Right: Bold Front. Early 20th-century design had settled down to the conventional layout by about 1905 – but the one area left for the designer's imagination was the front end. This picture shows the solid Teutonic radiator grille and brass cladding of the 1910 Adler.

Another bold front: The coal-scuttle décor of the 1913 Renault.

The Greek-temple styling of the front of the truly English Alldays, a company that clearly had aspirations of Rolls-Royce altitude.

15,000,000 of them made over 19 years, working on road and field, hill and track, used to milk cows (with suitable attachments!), to thresh wheat, to fell trees, to take the drummer and the doctor on their rounds, to transport the midwife to her patient's happy event – were so popular that some six years after the first one rolled off the assembly line, Henry Ford was making half the cars produced in the United States with just one-sixth of the work force. 'Without a doubt', eulogized one dealer, 'the greatest creation in automobiles ever placed before a people!' Whatever we may think today of the men that gave the world wheels, it must be appreciated that when the Model T first hit the road, it was a godsend to an upsurging nation of farmers and cattlemen and steelworkers – most of them former Europeans – who were desperate to wring a decent standard of living out of the hard earth. And motor transport cut down wasted travel time.

America needed the Model T – the high ground-clearance, the sizeable 2·9-litre powered unit, the rugged vanadium steel chassis, the simple no-nonsense superstructure. This was no rich man's toy as cars were considered to be in the 'Old Country'. Anything that cost $850 was going to be put to work.

Even the renowned Cadillac and the popular Buick of the time were typically American in that they showed, as the horse fraternity would have put it, a lot of daylight underneath. This, coupled with their generally larger engine capacity and overall build, lent U.S. cars a character of their own.

Olds, for example, had by this time, 1908, produced the powerful Model M (priced at a heady $2,750 and clothed in what was grandly called 'Palace Touring' bodywork) in the heavy U.S. style which at this end of the market was up to European price standards. This model, itself, led to that most famous of all Oldsmobile models, the legendary 'Limited'.

The 1910 Limited may not have been quite as suave as some of the transatlantic examples of the day (they now had doors to the front seats and high level sides, and were called torpedoes) but it was a winner. With a

Right: Henry Ford's ubiquitous Model T. It has vanadium steel in the right places, a 2·9-litre motor – and plenty of daylight underneath.

Electric automobiles had a long vogue, directed at Madam's shopping requirements in urban areas. This advertisement for the U.S. Rauch & Lang and Baker companies of 1916 shows the false bonnet containing the batteries, and describes rightly the ease of control. However, it omits to mention the maximum speed (about 17 mph) and the range limit (approximately 50 miles).

whopping great 707-cubic inch (11·58-litre) six-cylinder unit and enormous wheels with a base of 130 inches, the car was majestic. And with a relaxed cruising speed of between 60 and 70 mph it was a long-legged traveller.

At the same time Cadillac offered a four-cylinder tourer at $1,600, the Packard '30' had an upper-bracket following, and the prestigious Peerless marketed a fine six-cylinder.

Even steam was not yet dead in the U.S.A. and had a specialist following. Americans had flirted with steam since the 19th century, and the early days of gasoline power had dimmed their enthusiasm not a puff. Two major marques supplied a small but loyal steamer market: Stanley and White. One other U.S. steamer must be mentioned here: the Doble. This was a later contribution, a superbly engineered car produced from about 1914 to the surprisingly recent date of 1932. The trouble was that Abner Doble was too much of a perfectionist to make cars in quantity. His sophisticated vehicle with its four-cylinder 75-hp engine that would cruise silently at high speeds and climb hills with effortless ease, attracted Hollywood stars and royalty from Europe and India, but, sadly, production could not meet demand. Doble later came to England to work as a consultant to steam locomotive companies.

Two other milestones of U.S. automotive history were passed during the period 1906 until the U.S. entry to the First World War in 1917. French-Swiss immigrant Louis Chevrolet, who had come to the U.S. to promote sales of his wine-pump, drove in a motor race, attracted the attention of the ubiquitous Billy Durant, was engaged as team driver for Buick, and designed the first model of a new car, the Chevrolet Classic Six. The other development was perhaps more significant, for it radically changed the attitude of a large section of the public towards motoring.

Women had long been at a disadvantage in the motoring world due to their more delicate build. Swinging a starting-handle could injure a strong man if wrist and ignition happened to be misplaced, and ladies were certainly debarred from cranking all but the smallest of light cars. There were few women motorists in the early part of the century.

Charles Kettering, while working for the National Cash Register Company, developed a small electric motor that could give a short spurt of power, a jolt violent enough to shoot open the drawer of a cash register when a transaction was made. This motor was just the type Kettering needed to

power a pinion that could be flung forward to engage with the flywheel of a car and continue turning it just enough for the first sparking of the ignition. The first electric starters, made by Kettering's Delco Laboratories, were fitted on Cadillac cars from 1912, together with Delco electric lighting and ignition.

Private motoring was immediately opened to lady drivers in a way never before possible. But the electric starter did much more than put women behind the steering wheel.

Firstly, dress styles changed. Long voluminous skirts, which could get tangled in the gear lever and other bits and pieces disappeared. Dress length shortened. Now too, young women could drive from town to town to visit friends – without an escort. In both Europe and North America, country house weekends, house parties, shopping jaunts to town were possible for single ladies. If female fashion was the first thing to be changed by the woman at the wheel, then attitudes to travel, to work, to men, to just about every aspect of female life soon followed.

CADS AND SCORCHERS

The self-starter did not initially assume such great importance in Europe as in the U.S.A. After all, what were the servants for? This was a vastly different world from the U.S.A. Although the scene at London's Hyde Park Corner in the Edwardian days around 1909 (always the pulse of progress and fashion) had changed from the packed queues of Hansom cabs and growlers that earlier observations would have shown, now that taxi-cabs, motor buses and delivery vans were beginning to replace the horse in great numbers, motoring was still a leisure or sporting activity for the rich.

And motors were still frowned upon by many European countries. The last of the entrenched equestrians continued to expound their apoplectic anti-motoring views; and the common man too (or as often as not his wife, whose Monday washing line could be ruined by the clouds of dust raised by a passing car) was not yet eager to see motor transport take over the burdens of the horse, in whose welfare and industry many were engaged and from which he earned his daily bread. Furthermore, with his average wage of £2 a week, the little man's chances of owning one of these motorized magic carpets were limited to say the least. Nevertheless, 90,000 cars were registered in Great Britain by 1909, and, to the dismay of the French industry who

Above: M'lady still has her chauffeur in this Daimler poster from Germany. The self-starter, perhaps the major single advance that changed the face of motoring, was not yet needed in Europe.

Top: A 1913 Metz Model 22 two-seater from Waltham, Massachusetts. One of the early models of the first kit-car systems arrived in 14 packages, to be assembled at home. This model was delivered in the normal manner however.

Before the electric self-starter introduced women to popular motoring, dresses were fashionably long and voluminous. Once women took the driving seat, they shortened rapidly for sound practical reasons. This is an Austin York 40-hp landaulette made from 1907 until 1912.

had considered itself the leader of the automotive industrial world, only 38,000 were registered in France. They were losing the lead at last – and to Britain of all nations!

The British were experiencing their old legal problems again. Though the speed limit had been raised 20 mph in 1903 and most larger cars could travel at 50 mph day in, day out, tyres and road surfaces permitting, the cat-and-mouse games with the police and their cunning speed traps were still being played on the roads of England.

It must be admitted that some motorists of the day were pretty dreadful cads; this little verse, for instance, was supposed to be humorous:

'I collided with some trippers in my swift De Dion Bouton
Squashed them out as flat as kippers, left them *aussi mort que mouton*
What a nuisance trippers are, I must now repaint the car . . .'

Pedestrians could be equally dangerous. A few years earlier motoring journalist Dorothy Levitt (one of the women pioneers of pre-electric-starter days) recommended that: 'If you are to drive alone on the highways and byways it is advisable to carry a small revolver. I have an automatic Colt and find it easy to handle as there is practically no recoil. . . .' Sadly, her advice sounds all too modern. But perhaps a ladies' all-weather mask and the famous Scott spring-belt robe (the former looked very like a First World

War gas mask, and the latter like a Crusader's suit of mail) would probably have rendered the lady driver bullet-proof and her appearance so terrifying that any pioneer mugger would have taken to his heels at first acquaintance. As *Punch* put it:

> 'But what is this? What is this of sea or land?
> Female of sex it seems,
> That so bedecked, ornate and gay,
> Comes this way, sailing
> Like a stately ship . . .
> An amber scent of odoriferous perfume
> Her harbinger . . .'

Advice on motoring clothes abounded. Hats and protective masks were necessary in summer and winter, or passengers could end their journey looking like millers or mudlarks; some of the protective clothing was so bizarre it would have made space invaders look like choirboys.

But the motoring girl had to sacrifice elegance to sporting activity. One journalist wrote, 'Ladies must relinquish hope of keeping their soft peach-like bloom. The best remedy is cold water and a rough towel before you start', and 'With the help of the hot-water tin or, if that not be fitted . . . an ordinary hot-water bag, warm and at ease, one enjoys the pleasures provided by the ever-willing motor. . . .' That last piece of advice conveys clearly the miseries of motoring on a fine bright morning that turned to rain – the large flat windscreen failing to keep out the gusting storm, a flapping hood that served only to funnel the wet wind over the passengers. . . . With her large hat wrapped and strapped around her head, her Grand-Guignol mask enveloping her frozen face, clutching her soaking rainwear to her bosom and trying desperately to find a flicker of warmth from the hot-water tin at her feet, grandmother must indeed have been an iron butterfly.

TRAPPERS IN BLUE

The 'running' battle with the police continued well into the Edwardian era as the safe cruising speeds of cars rapidly increased while speed limits rose only slowly. A contemporary scribe wrote:

> 'Ware the peeler; see him stand
> Sneaking at milestones, watch in hand
> To swear your pace exceeded far
> The pace that's lawful to a car. . . .'

The Automobile Association was formed in Britain in 1905 with just two cyclist 'scouts' who patrolled the London-Brighton road; their job was to

Weather protection in the shape of a large windscreen, cart hood and vestigial side doors shows the advance of personal comforts. This is a De Dion-Bouton of 1911.

An early Torpedo. A straight (or nearly straight) line from the bonnet – or hood – through the tops of the doors was an attempt to tidy up the somewhat ragged look of the automobile in about 1911. It was this design that caused some later cars to look like upturned bathtubs on wheels. This neat little Opel achieved a dainty profile. It was developed into the 'Puppchen' (Dolly) model of 1912 that proved extremely popular in Germany.

warn motorists of police speed traps. The organization grew into a nationwide patrol system, whose aims were mainly to assist the motorist whose car had suffered a breakdown and also to stop and supply passing members with information about traps ahead. The police, only doing their duty as laid down by the law, sometimes stealthily moved a trap so that the AA man was actually standing inside a trapping zone. In that way he was breaking the law and could be prosecuted. The AA retaliated by telling members that 'If the Patrolman does not salute (it had been normal practice), STOP and ask the reason.' The patrolman would then privately inform the member of a 'hazard' a mile or two ahead.

The AA man was so successful in supporting its members against police harassment, that some 12,000 motorists had joined by 1909. And although there was a small number of 'scorchers' who raced madly about at 30 or even 40 mph, raising vast trails of dust, most who owned motor vehicles were responsible people who were happy enough to enjoy their new Rover or Vauxhall at speeds below the statutory limit.

As motoring increased in popularity, police duties also multiplied. The 'sport' of speed-trapping gave way to other traffic duties of a less controversial nature. AA scouts and the police began to work together to the same ends. By 1912 the AA was so respectable that included in its 43,000 members were the Archbishop of Canterbury, the Prime Minister, almost half the Royal Family (the other half were in the Royal Automobile Club), and that noisy young politician, W. S. Churchill.

In some other countries a similar guerrilla war was being waged in pre-war days against authorities and their 19th century attitude. For instance, Austria had a city-street speed limit of 10 km/h (6 mph) over bridges and near towns. Belgium, however, allowed 50 km/h (31 mph) except in Brussels. Only in France, with its long straight roads from Napoleon's days and earlier, was there no speed limit at all, a veritable motorist's Elysium.

In the U.S.A. individual States' regulations varied considerably. By 1905 most of them had formulated laws which they considered would compel citizens to drive within their local safety limits. The most liberal, with a 'country' limit of 25 mph, were Wisconsin, Minnesota and Michigan. Most of the others had a 15 mph top speed, and something in the region of 6 mph in towns, on bends, near dams, at crossroads and so on. In fact, it mattered little what the country limit was set at – most surfaces would have shattered something vital at anything over a trotting pace. One comment of the day, a newspaper snippet, says it all. 'Citizens of Danville cannot travel to Mount Morris, 15 miles away, during the spring for the road is impassable, as the broken down waggons and buggies that line the road from end to end bear mute witness.'

THE LAST GOLDEN DAYS

Edwardian days ended in 1910, but there was a period immediately following the King's death, a sort of hiatus in history, that lasted a few more golden years before the lifestyle, peculiar to royal Bertie's time, was swept away forever by war.

Motoring had still not taken – in Europe at least – its now-familiar place as the normal universal transport for all classes of users, but the days when the rest of the world looked at milady in awe through the plateglass windows of her motor carriage were ending.

A small band of enthusiasts, the first do-it-yourself buffs of the motor world, were starting to put together flimsy cars of their own – cyclecars – a new word in the motoring lexicon but one that unhappily often indicated that the fragile vehicles combined the worst properties of both car and cycle. However, some of them, manufactured at commercial level, were worthy of note. The light and simple GN made by A. Frazer-Nash and H. R. Godfrey was typical of one that improved with its maker's experience. This vehicle at first comprised a wooden-frame chassis with a tiny twin-cylinder air-cooled motor with transmission by V-belts and pulleys. By the Twenties it was made at a rate of about 50 a week. GN became a respected marque as steel chassis replaced wood, steering box supplanted wire-and-bobbin, and handling improved. This little car actually became renowned for its sporting performance, its simplicity of maintenance and its economy, which was, of course, the prime reason for the original emergence of this type of spartan vehicle.

Numbers of 'New Motoring' wire-and-bobbin vehicles were made just before the First World War: France had its Bedélia, a curious rear-seat-piloted coffin-shaped torpedo, and the aptly-named Violet Bogey; and

Modest motoring. One of the best Edwardians of its type, this 1913 10-hp Clement-Bayard two-seater has a four-cylinder side-valve unit of 1354 cc and, like its contemporary Renault, a scuttle bonnet and dashboard radiator.

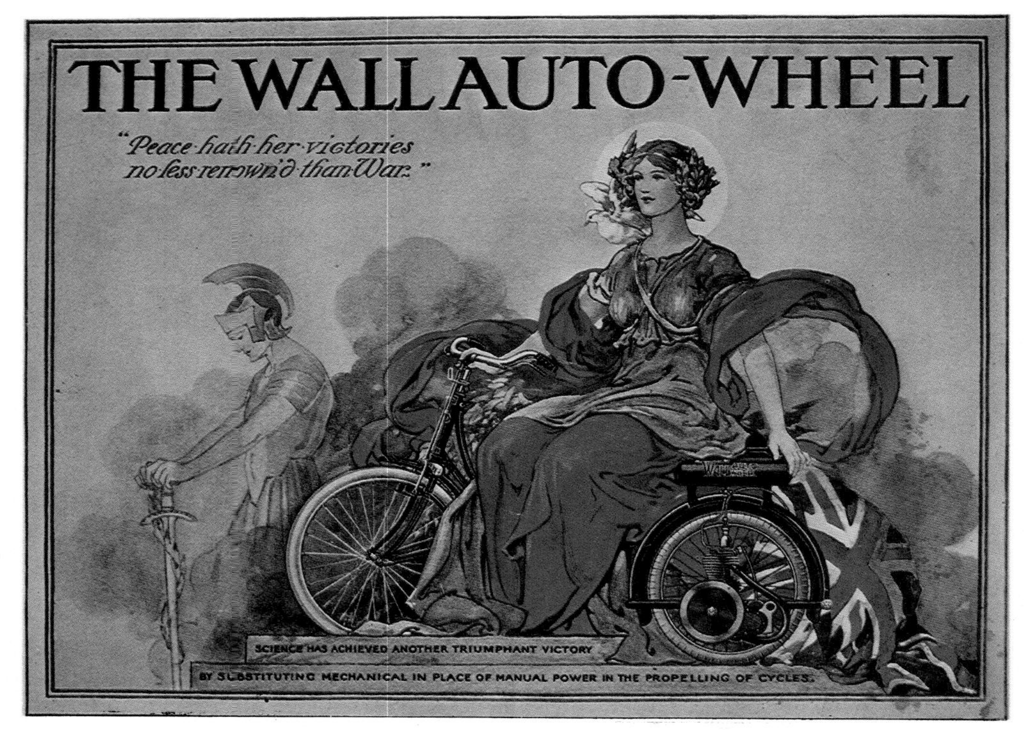

Right: 'Swap your pedals for a Wall Auto-Wheel', said the advertisement – in the turgid prose style of the time. This 1914 piece of classic Britannic artwork shows the wheel preparatory to installation. The Roman soldier clearly doubts that a tiny single-cylinder air-cooled coffee percolator will get him anywhere.

A GN at speed during a vintage car race. Longest-lived of British cycle cars, the London-region-built GN first used a bought-in 1000-cc engine, but the company soon began to make their own. From a typical cycle-car product the firm graduated to sturdy if light vehicles that made their name in competition during the Twenties – and still win vintage races today.

Britain had its GN, Morgan, GWK (friction drive by a disc of compressed paper!). Some survived the brief postwar boom, but cyclecars, already a declining genre in the early Twenties, received their *coup-de-grâce* in 1922 when Herbert Austin brought out his diminutive Seven. Although the Seven was as small as many cyclecars, it had all the attributes of a full-size motor car, accommodating up to four (smallish) occupants rather than the two that could be shoe-horned into a cyclecar.

France's other light car of the last years of peace was the equally small (but never classed as a cyclecar) Peugeot Bébé of 1912. Designed by Ettore Bugatti, this too had a two-seater layout, a 6-hp 855-cc engine, and a wheelbase of just around 2·5 metres (98·5 inches). The delightfully big-car Bébé proved popular with the impecunious, and was made in quantity during the last years of dilettante motoring.

These were also years of steady refinement for the automobile: electric headlamps were taking over from malodorous acetylene (and causing considerable dazzle before focusing was understood); various types of valves were being tried as alternatives to poppet valves, the most dramatic perhaps being the rotary valves of the Italian Itala and the newly popular sleeve-valve introduced by Charles Knight and used by Daimler and others. In Britain racing at Brooklands was the chic thing and added much to the knowledge of brakes, tyres, sustained high speeds, handling and first-aid.

Motoring costs were coming *down*. Top people were queueing for Rolls-Royce cars – and waiting up to three months even for the chassis. Young Oxford garage-proprietor W. R. Morris was designing a new small car with a White & Poppe engine that he was to offer the public in 1913 – the Morris Oxford.

The life and career of William Morris, later Lord Nuffield, has often been described as 'the greatest success story of the century', and in England it was, indeed, a unique story of energy, business acumen, timing – and Bill Morris' winning smile. His first Oxfords housed 10-hp splash-lubricated side-valve 1-litre units, and were assembled at the 'Oxford Motor Palace', as his smart new works were called. Morris' first car soon proved to be the best British light car made at the time, and at £175 was the right price for modest pockets (50 mph and 50 mpg said the ads). He sold 1,000 in the first year. By 1915 he had made a larger version, the Cowley, and at this date both models used U.S. Continental engines.

By the end of this golden period of motoring the shape, the fuel and ignition systems, drive train and so on of most cars had settled into the pattern that remained constant for 50 years; motoring itself was on the brink of common acceptance. Chain drive had vanished. Self-starters were the rule rather than the exception. Four-wheel brakes were beginning to appear. Steel pistons were seen and four-speed gearboxes were normal. Carburation had improved greatly over the past couple of years. Safety glass was being specified by more purchasers. Coachwork had begun to reflect modern art: no longer seen were the iron curliques and filigrees of horse-carriage days; the more slender lines of air-piercing architecture were beginning to appear. The use of aluminium allowed the functional sweep of body-design that took the art forward another step, and the open touring or torpedo bodies of the 1920s could incipiently be seen. Even the chauffeur now had some protection as the closed brougham or coupe-de-ville was extended to cover the man at the wheel.

The war that was to engulf Europe in 1914, and the U.S.A. in 1917, was to augment the increasing sophistication and proliferation of the automobile in the way, sadly, that all wars stimulate technical progress more effectively than the less desperate needs of peace. The mass invasion of the automobile and its profound influence on our lifestyle was fast approaching.

William Morris built one of the largest companies in British motor history. This is the first car he offered for sale in 1913, a 1018-cc Morris Oxford.

The Lure of Speed

The earliest motorsport events, held in France, were, in effect, trials of reliability. That an automobile could actually reach a destination 50 km (31 miles) distant brought praise indeed for the vehicle, its maker and its *conducteur*, whether it was competing for a prize at the end of the voyage, or journeying to visit Grandma.

Very shortly after the first self-propelled cars wheezed along the roads of Mannheim or Paris or Brussels in the early 1890s, their owners, mostly French at this time, dreamed up a *concours*, a competition between their vehicles.

The first genuine sporting competition was the Reliability Trial of 1894 from Paris to Rouen, mounted by news-chief Pierre Giffard of *Petit-Journal*, which introduced a lasting spirit of competition into motoring. It needed very little to persuade the young bucks of France to take up the sport – the small côterie of *automobilistes* could hardly wait for the next contest and fixed an ambitious event for 13 June the following year.

The 1895 Paris-Bordeaux-Paris race netted other sponsors in addition to the pioneering magazine, *Petit-Journal*, and the entry was impressive. Some 22 hopefuls drove an assortment of vehicles including six Bollée steamers, 13 *voitures à petrole*, two motorcycles and a single Jentaud electric. The gasoline cars were from the stables of Panhard et Levassor, Peugeot (both using Daimler engines) and Benz. It was to be a long, hard race, with tight regulations stating that repairs could be effected only by such means as could be carried on the car, and that nothing outside was to be procured except as 'entertainment for man and machine'. The total length of 1,178 km (732 miles) was a cosmic distance in those times and allowance was made for changing drivers en route.

A report mentions in passing that the Michelin brothers, in their Peugeot No. 46, demonstrated, in public for the first time, an auto which did not roll on '*bandages classiques*' (iron-shod wheels) or on solid rubber but on air. The car, says the report, was named 'Eclair' (Lightning) not because of its high speed but because of its zig-zag progress!

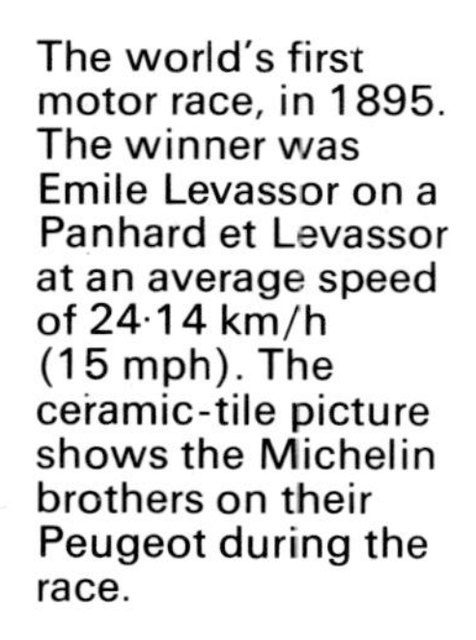

The world's first motor race, in 1895. The winner was Emile Levassor on a Panhard et Levassor at an average speed of 24·14 km/h (15 mph). The ceramic-tile picture shows the Michelin brothers on their Peugeot during the race.

In 1899 this electric car (now at the Musée de l'Automobile at Compiègne in France) held the world land speed record at 105·88 km/h (65·79 mph).

Emile Levassor won this first genuine race, at an average of 24·47 km/h (15·2 mph) on his solid-tyred Panhard et Levassor and if this were not dramatic enough, he wrote his name in the halls of fame by driving the whole way himself.

Levassor had driven away from the Versailles startline at the Place d'Armes around noon, pointed his car southwest and plugged along the dusty roads through the Loire and the Charente regions to Bordeaux on a first leg of 586 km (366 miles).

Bumping down the long straight main street of Ruffec he arrived at the house of his relief driver. However, Levassor was so far ahead of his schedule that he had reached the town in the small hours, and found that his relief driver was still in bed. He continued to Bordeaux alone, still reasonably fresh.

Arriving at the seaport town at around 10 am Levassor turned his V-twin two-seater Panhard round, and started back for Paris. This time his No. 2 was wide awake and waiting at Ruffec to take over. However, the 52-year-old driver waved him away. He drove on through the day and night (his lighting system falling off at some point) shouting greetings to other competitors that he met still chugging down to Bordeaux.

Levassor arrived at the Porte Maillot in Paris some six hours ahead of his nearest rival. He was flagged in, congratulated, fêted, and while he was having a light breakfast of champagne and a couple of poached eggs, he was disqualified: his car had only two seats instead of the four required by the regulations. Levassor's victory was no less significant for that, and he is still recorded in motoring history as the victor of the first motor *race*, with a fine monument to his feat erected at the Porte Maillot.

Soon motor races were crossing international frontiers, and the brief period of marathon capital-to-capital contests drew competitors from countries on both sides of the Atlantic.

The U.S.A. entered motorsport in 1895 when the *Chicago Times-Herald* sponsored a race of 94 miles and attracted almost a hundred entrants.

Publisher H. H. Kohlstat was overjoyed at the publicity, but as the day drew nearer he began to realize that most of his 'competitors' were backyard optimists whose engineering lagged a long way behind their aspirations. The planned July date was changed to November and the route shortened from Chicago to Evanstown, 54 miles away. Six cars lined up on a chill and slushy day. Two electric cars sat silently on the Midway Plaisance startline, praying their batteries stayed unfrozen; a Duryea, the first real All-American car, slithered about the roadway, and a couple of Benz cars and a French Roger coughed and gasped in front of an early morning crowd.

There were several squabbles about who won on which vehicle, but the reportage of the day leaves us all somewhat in a fog about the results. German history would, no doubt, list the only surviving Benz as the winner, while local reports have favoured the Duryea. It mattered not a jot – the U.S. had joined the sporting world, and was to play an important role in it in the years to follow.

Another signpost to the future direction of automotive technology was seen in the 1902 Paris-Vienna race. On a course that necessitated drivers lashing themselves to their foot-pedals in order to stay in the car as it rocketed over incredibly rough alpine tracks, a large car was confidentally expected to win. When Marcel Renault won in his small car, so far ahead of the vastly more powerful motors of the opposition that the officials at the finishing-line in Vienna simply did not believe that this was indeed Marcel Renault, the competitor from France, it pointed inexorably to the use of smaller engines. However, it was to take half-a-dozen years for most manufacturers to realize that greater literage was not the best way to increase power and efficiency.

OPEN ROAD TO CLOSED CIRCUIT

With the disastrous Paris-Madrid race of 1903, terminated after the first leg to stop the slaughter, speed competition was taken off the main roads of Europe and run on circuits, either on closed public roads or, as in the case of Brooklands in England and Indianapolis in the U.S., on tracks specifically designed for motor racing.

The 1906 French Grand Prix, held at Le Mans (although not on today's circuit), created a sensation as the first major race held on a large closed-road circuit at which, the crowd soon realized, one could safely watch the cars race repeatedly round the track from a single vantage-point.

A 1902 Serpollet steam-powered racing vehicle of the type that competed in the 1903 Paris-Madrid race, last of the early capital-to-capital speed events. It is now at the Schlumf Museum at Mulhouse in France.

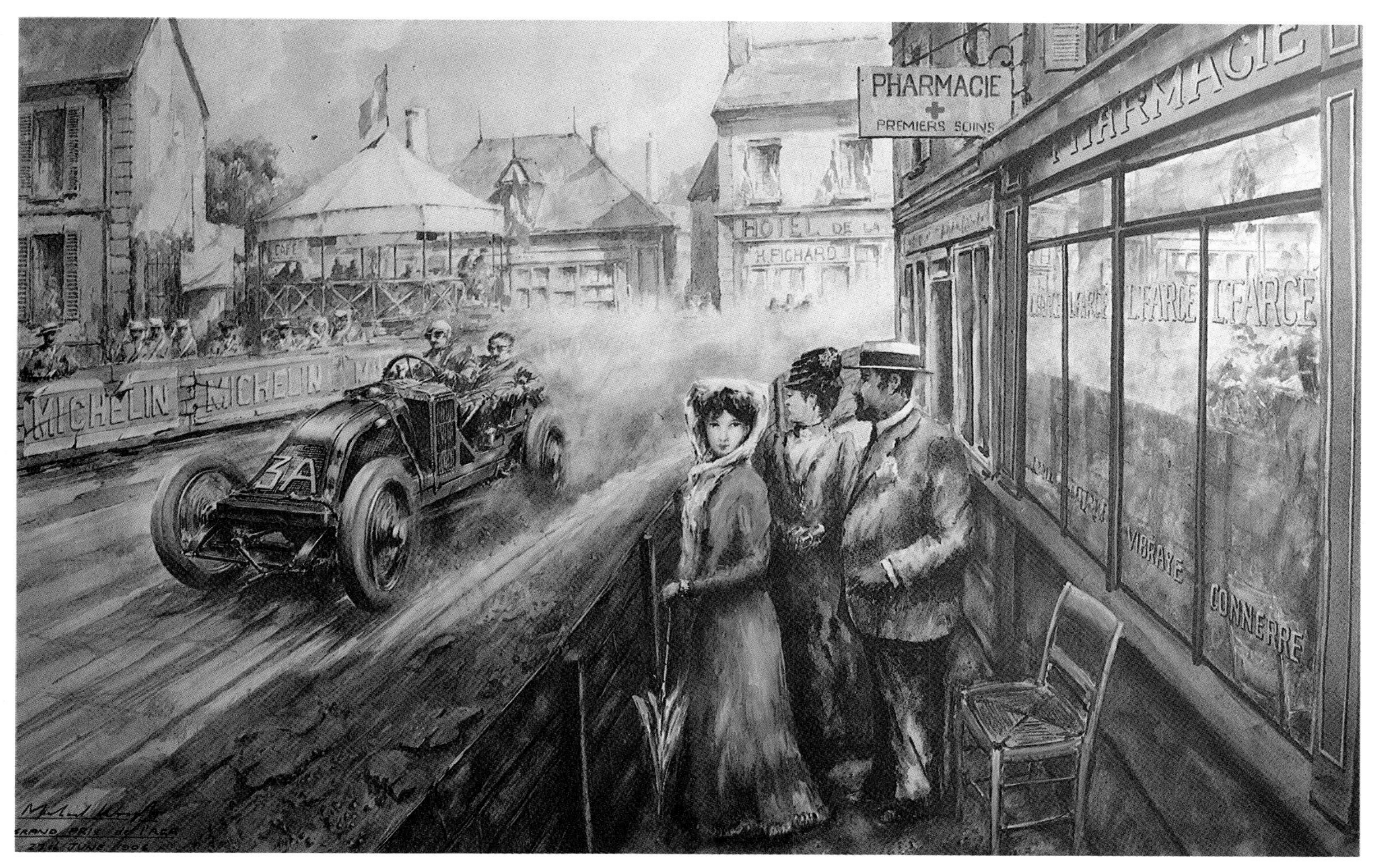

The first genuine Grand Prix run on a closed circuit took place in 1906 at a long circuit at Le Mans. It was won by this Renault powered by a 13-litre engine. (Painting by Michael Wright.)

From 1906 until 1914 Grand Prix motor racing was run under regulations drawn up by the A.C.F. (Automobile Club de France). Below are the main regulations for Grand Prix racing in those early years.

1906	1,000 kilogrammes maximum weight of car
1907	Maximum fuel consumption 3·3 km/l (9·4 mpg)
1908	Maximum piston area 755 sq cm (117 sq in)
1912	Free Formula (Formula Libre)
1913	Maximum fuel consumption 5 km/l (14·2 mpg)
1914	Maximum engine capacity 4·5 litres unsupercharged
1921	Maximum engine capacity 3 litres
1922–25	Maximum engine capacity 2 litres
1926–27	Maximum engine capacity 1·5 litres
1928–33	Various fuel and structure regulations, leaving engine capacity unlimited. In effect, a free formula.

The spectacle of early Grand Prix racing led to the establishing of several other races, perhaps the most lasting of which was a round-the-mountains event organized by Sicilian Vincenzo Florio. Florio had owned one of the first cars on the rugged island of Sicily. As chauffeur he employed a young driver, Felice Nazzaro, who was also driving for the Fiat team in various races, and winning (often in competition with his friend and rival Vincenzo Lancia). Florio wanted to stage a race of his own, a tough rough-road race over the dangerous mountain roads of Sicily. The first was run in 1906, but not without some 'small' but significant snags. For example, during practice, competitors were pot-shot at by the local banditti. The moving cars presented, it seemed, an irresistible target for the men of the mountains. Florio's solution pleased everybody. He co-opted the most troublesome of the brigands as official race stewards. Oldest and most romantic of the endurance races, the Targa remained in the calendar for many years, and although the cars seen in the Seventies pounding over the still-dangerous Sicilian mountain roads were very different from the Fiats and Italias of early days, its unique character has remained.

A giant 130-hp Fiat Corsa (racing car) roaring round the circuit during one of the three major races of 1907. Fiat won them all that year. (Painting by Dion Pears.)

The 1908 French Grand Prix was won by a 12·8-litre Mercedes driven by former locksmith Christian Lautenschlager for Germany. This wall-tile picture is one of a historic series that may be seen outside the Michelin Tyre Company's building in London.

The Indianapolis Motor Speedway, America's vast banked rectangular circuit (later dubbed the 'Brickyard'), was opened in 1911. This is an artist's impression – only a little exaggerated – of an early race.

This 12·8-litre chain-driven 1908 Panhard Grand Prix car was one of the last of the giants. The French company had fielded cars of up to 18·3 litres in an effort to win earlier races.

Of the two other 'classic' endurance races, Italy's Mille Miglia and the Twenty-four Hours of Le Mans held in the Sarthe region of France, only Le Mans survives.

The 'Thousand Miles of Italy', inspired by the success of the Targa Florio, was to be a car-breaking marathon round the northern half of the Italian peninsula. The race included long stretches of fast road, Alpine passes, winding hills and, toughest of all, twisting dashes through the main streets of some of the great cities, including Rome. Legend soon surrounded the race, the cars, and the winners – mainly Italian at first – who became national heroes, fêted and sure of lasting fame. The Mille Miglia victors' list resounds with names like Campari, Ramponi, Nuvolari, Varzi, Biondetti, Marzotto and one or two 'intruders' like Caracciola (German) and Stirling Moss (British). Moss's win in 1955 was undoubtedly the greatest of all time, and certainly the fastest. He drove his Mercedes 300SLR single-handed for the entire race to win at a speed that was never exceeded.

Le Mans is something quite different. Since 1923, Le Mans has been a 'Derby' day outing for the people of France. Sports fans, campers, lovers, families turn up to watch (or as often as not, not to bother to watch) the 24 hours of racing. Fairgrounds and bars keep them happy through the night and long grass shelters their sleeping forms during the last hours of the contest. But more of this race later.

END OF AN EPOCH

As early as 1902 a small car had beaten the multiple-litre monsters to the post. The 3·7-litre Renault, driven by Marcel of that name, left its jumbo rivals in the dust as he drove across the Continent from Paris to Vienna, but the lesson he taught that day was not reflected in Grand Prix Formula rules until 1914, when the regulations were redesigned to control engine capacities. The Grand Prix of 1914 (there was still only one genuine Grand Prix – the French one – although there were other excellent events that drew large entries and crowds, such as the Vanderbilt Cup, the Indianapolis 500, the Tourist Trophy on the Isle of Man, the Austrian Alpine Trials and so on) was run under the rules that limited engine size to an unsupercharged 4·5 litres.

Right: German Mercedes driver Lautenschlager was the victor of the French Grand Prix again in 1914, in a race that was to mark the end of an epoch. The Mercedes drivers worked as a single team unit to capture the prize, having planned to tempt other drivers into indiscretions by setting a too-fast pace with a 'decoy' car.

The Grand Prix de l'A.C.F. (French Grand Prix) was revived in 1912 after a lapse of two years. The two-day 956-mile race was won by the new Henry-designed Peugeot driven by Georges Boillot, a *pilote* who was to become France's favourite. The twin-overhead-camshaft four-cylinder 16-valve Peugeot of 1908 is today recognized as the first of the modern racing cars. The poster was inaccurate – only 47 cars took part.

The year marked the end of an epoch in the world of motorsport as well as in other worlds. And once again Mercedes was the catalyst, just as it was when it made its first appearance at Nice 13 years earlier and just as it was to be 40 years later when Mercedes-Benz returned to Grand Prix racing in 1954 with the 2·5-litre straight-eight Silver Arrow, to win everything in sight in the following couple of years.

The Hispano-Suiza inspired Peugeot, designed by Ernest Henry in 1912, had twin overhead camshafts, four cylinders and 16 valves (at a time when competitors such as Vauxhall and Sunbeam were still using the venerable side-valve) and had taken first place in the 1912 and 1913 Grands Prix in the skilled hands of George Boillot, who, at 29, was France's national favourite.

The race started with 41 cars on the line; competitors were flagged off in pairs every half minute, making the progress of the race a complex mathematical exercise. The French crowds were restless during the first lap of 23 miles, but when their man, Boillot, came pounding round the grandstand bend in the apparent lead, their delight knew no bounds. However, when Mercedes driver, Sailer, appeared a few moments later, and a quick spot of arithmetic showed that he was, in fact, leading the race by 18 seconds, they became silent and apprehensive. With two other leaders, a Sunbeam and a Delage, the race soon seemed to develop into a four-cornered affair, but the field had reckoned without the wily tactics of the Mercedes team drivers.

When Sailer in Mercedes No. 14 began to trail the blue wasp-tailed Peugeot, Boillot was stung into taking corners at break-neck speed, trusting that his four-wheel brakes would out-perform the rear-wheels-only brakes of the Mercedes car. They did, and Boillot was triumphant. Little did he know that it was part of a plan to force up the pace [speeds were up to 118 mph (190 km/h) on faster parts of the circuit], and that the two other German cars were following in a loose convoy behind, waiting for Sailer to push Boillot into an indiscretion. The plan worked, but not before Boillot had seen Sailer's Mercedes forced out with a broken crankshaft. Then the Peugeot's differential began to make ominous noises. He slowed down. Mercedes No. 28 with Lautenschlager at the wheel slipped past into the lead, where it stayed until the final flag.

The Mercedes win in this 20-lap race offered several salutary lessons to drivers and constructors. But another contest intervened, and motor engineering moved rapidly to a war footing. The gallant Boillot, who had become a pilot, was heard of only once again. On patrol over enemy lines he encountered three German planes of a hunting *geschwader*. Discretion would have suggested withdrawal, but the Gallic Boillot was not of a cautious nature, and he accepted the challenge. He died that day in the wreckage of his aircraft.

Ettore Bugatti's racing cars of the Twenties scored over 2,000 sporting victories. This is the Type 35B of 1926 which has a 2262-cc supercharged power unit.

SPORTING TWENTIES

Somewhat overshadowed by the Mercedes win of 1914, several other constructors were fighting for sporting successes. Italian-born Bugatti had produced his Type 13, a compact 1·4-litre car that had already made its mark in motorsport; Fiat was still in the sport in 1914, although their *annus mirabilis* was back in 1907 when they won all three major races of the year. Panhard's salad days were also history but they, too, were still in the running. Opel, Vauxhall, Delage, Sunbeam, Alda, Peugeot – all had their sporting products on show at various competitions.

The French Grand Prix was again one of the most significant races of the early post-war period. Fred Duesenberg and brother August had been making cars for a long time and had formed their own company in 1913. When the war ended they began to build racing machines. In 1920 they captured the (unofficial) World Land Speed Record with a speed of

Vintage days revived. A Bentley 3-litre of 1924 negotiates a fast bend at Oulton Park, one of Britain's northern racing circuits.

156·05 mph at Daytona. And in 1921 a Duesenberg 3089-cc straight-eight Grand Prix car won the French Grand Prix. This rocked the sporting world – after all, anything that had *anything* to do with motor racing came from Europe. An American win turned the world of motorsport upside-down. Not only was Fred's car first in the race, and the first ever American win, but it was also the first win with four-wheel hydraulic brakes, the first win with engine in unit with the gearbox, the first win using a centrally-sited gear lever, and the first to race without carrying a spare wheel. The Duesenberg went on to become one of the coveted automobiles of the age, sought and bought by the rich and the famous. The car's price matched its performance however, and the S and SJ versions have a place in history as being larger, faster, and more expensive than any other American car of the time. In 1932, when the more powerful SJ was introduced, its top speed of 130 mph made it the most spectacular automobile in the U.S.A. The Duesenberg Motor Company had been absorbed into the Cord empire in 1926, and in 1937 ceased production. But the Duesenberg did not vanish forever. Today, faithful reproductions of the S and SJ are painstakingly being made in the U.S.A. and bought by eager collectors of classic cars.

The Grand Prix Formula was reduced in 1922 to 2 litres. Several Italian manufacturers started to take notice again after a devastating war.

In 1923 Alfa Romeo produced the first true Grand Prix car, the P1, but never raced it. A completely new car, the P2, was shown in 1924, a straight-eight supercharged 2 litre, which won its first race and dominated Grand Prix racing for the duration of the 2-litre Formula. (A single British success occurred during 1923. Henry Segrave won the French Grand Prix in a Sunbeam, a rare British 'double' win that was not repeated until British driver Tony Brooks won the Syracuse Grand Prix in 1955 in a British Connaught.)

Ettore Bugatti had unveiled his remarkable Type 35 by 1924, with its jewel-like eight-cylinder power unit that in fact had grown out of the somewhat unsuccessful Type 30 'Tank' Bugatti of 1923. Bugatti's car scored nearly 2,000 wins during the next few years on the racing circuits of the world.

In 1925 the regulation requiring on-board mechanics was abandoned, and a driving mirror became a vital accessory, although few drivers would admit to their usefulness. The 1·5-litre Formula that was introduced in 1926 brought a number of new entrants. The French Delage Grand Prix cars of that year were fine 1·5 straight-eights with twin superchargers, five-speed overdrive gearboxes, and a top speed of around 130 mph. They provided worthy competition for other racing marques: Bugatti, Alvis, Fiat, Talbot, Maserati, and Alfa Romeo. All Grand Prix entries used superchargers this year and for the duration of the Formula.

Opened in 1923, Le Mans has since become the best-known motor race in the world, although its character has changed considerably since the Twenties. It was originally designed as a race for normal production cars of the type that one could see on the boulevard or on the country roads every day. Each car entered had to be identical with 30 others that had been built for general catalogue purchases, and all cars over 1,100 cc had to be four-seaters. The day-night-day endurance event would be won by the car that had covered the greatest distance within the 24 hours. Not only was this a test of driving skills but a win would bring the searchlight of the most valuable kind of publicity down on the car's maker, giving a strong boost to

A 1926 Bentley 3/4·5-litre Le Mans two-seater Speed Model. It has four cylinders, overhead camshaft and water-cooled monoblock engine with 11-mm bore, 140-mm stroke and 4398-cc capacity, and is one of the most handsome sports cars still with a current licence.

sales. The public could understand an event that used vehicles and machinery with which many of them were already familiar, and they flocked to the Sarthe circuit.

The long race was very much a French benefit in its first year, but the title was captured by British Bentley drivers Duff and Clement in 1924. Bentley cars won Le Mans for four more years, 1927 to 1930, before surrendering to a succession of Alfa Romeo wins, but the Bentley 'legend' was born of the strange events on the night of the 1927 race. A multi-car crash at White House Corner had wrecked all the cars involved except the Bentley of British drivers Benjafield and Davies, who managed to get their car, No. 3, running and on the road again after side-swiping the pile-up. They limped off into the night with little hope of finishing. The fact that their half-wrecked car not only finished but won has passed into the folklore of motor sport.

The Twenties were the hey-day of truly amateur sportsmen when rallies had a touch of 'hock-and-hamper' picnic luxury, and motor racing a flavour of chivalrous rivalry. Drivers were household names, boys' heroes, and often leaders of society. What distinguished the vehicles of the Twenties from those of the next decade was their strong individual character, imprinted with the personalities of the men who had made them – Ford, Royce, Lancia, Vauxhall's Pomeroy, Bugatti the Maestro, Fred and August Duesenberg. Later sportscars may have out-performed them, modern racing cars may have out-engineered them, but the hand of their makers, from designer to hand-polisher, was part of the very fabric of the sporting vintage car, a quality that became noticeably less and less visible as the years moved on.

The Alfa Romeo P2. First seen in 1924, the P2, a straight-eight supercharged 2-litre car, dominated racing during the 2-litre formula.

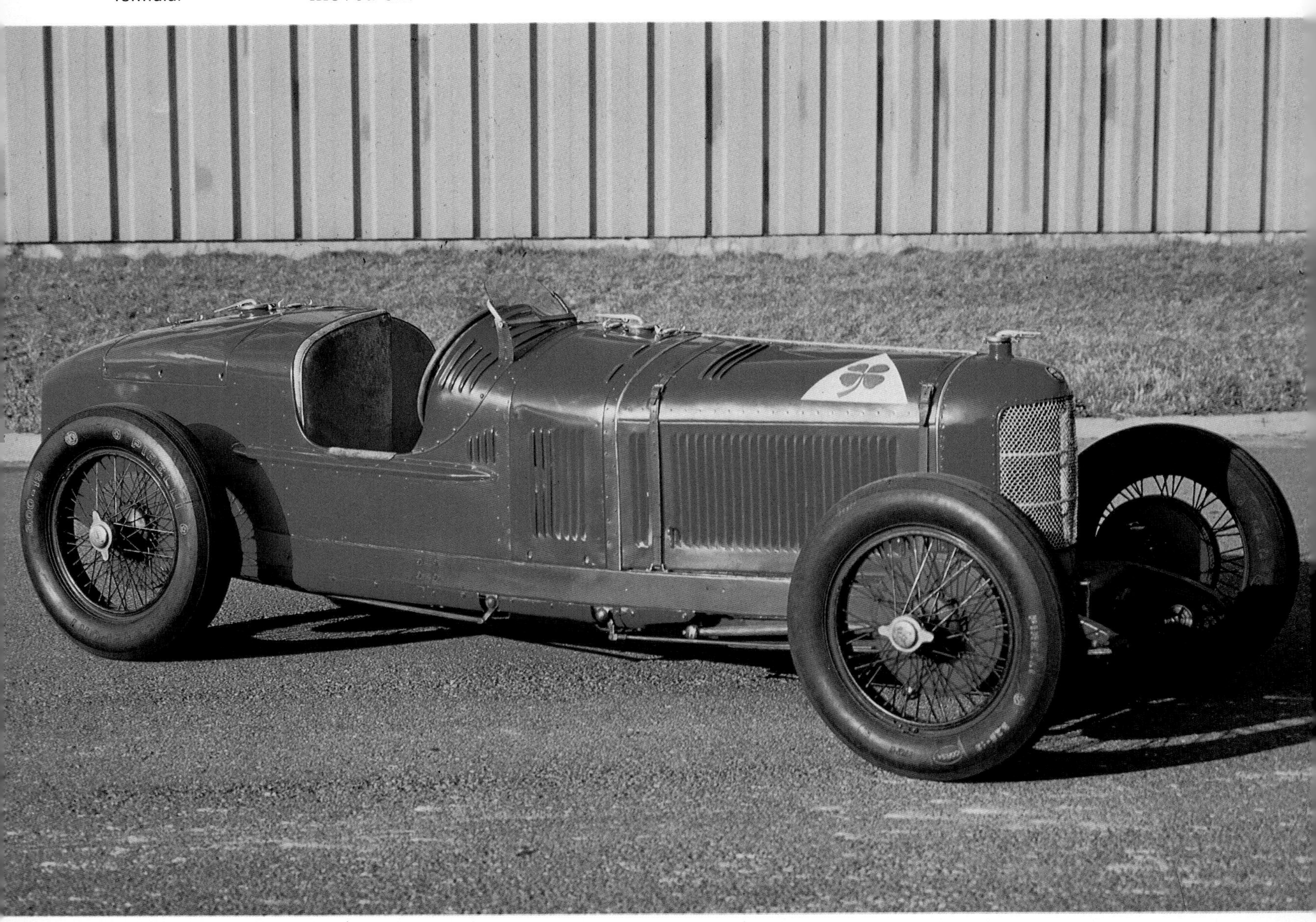

Those Vintage Years

The war that ended on a foggy November day in 1918 had taught automobile manufacturers a great deal about their job. Its decrees had forced the speeding-up of production, demanded improved methods of construction and the use of new alloys, and had fostered industrial co-operation. The aviation industry had been under the most pressure and had come up with some superb new engine designs.

The Hispano Suiza six-cylinder engine, seen in the first post-war car, was perhaps the finest example of the influence of wartime aero-engine development. Its overhead camshaft and light alloy block with steel liners gave it a top speed of 90 mph and a peak power of 135 bhp. Four-wheel brakes were essential now and the Hispano Suiza stopping mechanism was servo-assisted. Fitted to the French-built H6 chassis, it resulted in a car that arguably out-classed the current Rolls-Royce, which had not yet progressed beyond rear-wheel anchors and side valves.

If the Hispano set the post-war pace for those who could dig deep in their pocket, others were hurriedly turning – or returning – to peacetime work and aiming at a market that would serve homecoming heroes whose savings would be on a more modest scale.

War had razed more than the factories and homes of the French and the Belgians: it had demolished some of the inequalities between social classes – or at least their aspirations in the matter of transport. The 'poor man's gondola', the penny tramcar, was no longer acceptable to the man in the street. Although there was to be a recession in the early Twenties, the immediate post-war boom after four years of austerity encouraged many manufacturers to cobble up something, reasonably priced, on four wheels as quickly as possible.

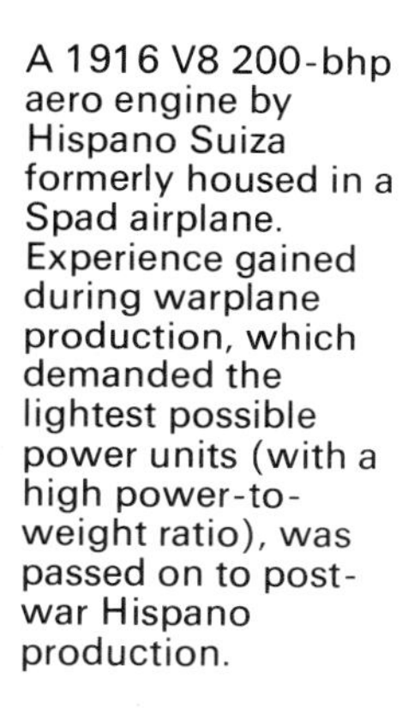

A 1916 V8 200-bhp aero engine by Hispano Suiza formerly housed in a Spad airplane. Experience gained during warplane production, which demanded the lightest possible power units (with a high power-to-weight ratio), was passed on to post-war Hispano production.

A 1921 Delage Type DE4, a handsome family car from a classic French marque. It is powered by a Boillot 2120-cc side-valve unit.

'WEST OF LARAMIE'

The U.S.A., relatively untouched by war, moved smoothly over to peacetime work and was soon offering re-vamped 1917 models to a public who knew there would be a three-year shortage of cars in the showrooms. The Kissel Gold Bug, a sporty yellow 4·3-litre speedster was popular. Auburn's streamlined Beauty Six appeared; the cheaply assembled Dixie Flyer from Kentucky was selling furiously; Hudson had made plans for producing 40,000 cars in the first post-war year – and achieved the astonishing figure.

'Back-to-business – fast!' was the maxim in the United States in 1919. The world's first three-colour traffic lights were seen in Detroit, a national coast-to-coast highway research programme was launched with motor travel in mind, experimental road surfaces were tested for the first time (there were just 191 miles of Federal-aided highway in the entire country at the time). Shapes were changing even if only in detail rather than in structure: sloping windshields were seen, front-and-rear bumpers were standard on several makes, balloon tyres were introduced, tourers (easier perhaps to produce than sedans) were popular. The automotive industry was moving quickly into the post-war market. The next year U.S. makers nudged the two million mark for the first time, and despite a recession in 1921, a shattering 3,624,717 cars were made in the U.S.A. in 1923.

A number of new manufacturers had mushroomed overnight, putting together cars with bought-in parts on a single assembly line. Many were attracted by the immediate post-war situation in the U.S.A. and many made cars that were no better than the next hopeful's product, but one or two caught the public's imagination and became the popular buy of the period. Most significant perhaps was the Jordan, made in Cleveland, Ohio, by former wartime air ace, Edward S. Jordan. His claim to a niche in history was not for the quality of his product – it was much the same as any 'assembled' automobile – but in the way he broke away from the dull technical 'nuts and bolts' advertising of the day to bring a new romantic, evocative style of writing into his promotional material.

Jordan's gimmick worked better than he could possibly have hoped. He sold his 'Playboy' with its 5-litre six-cylinder engine, wire-wheels and pleasant appointments with the help of the first 'poetry of the automobile', words that are reputed to hang still in every adman's office in Madison Avenue as a lesson in the art. Here is the best of his 'Playboy' copy:

> 'Somewhere west of Laramie there's a broncho-busting, steer-roping girl who knows what I'm talking about. She can tell what a sassy pony – that's a cross between greased lightning and the place where it hits – can do with eleven hundred pounds of steel and action when he's going high, wide and handsome.
> The truth is – the Playboy was built for her,
> Built for the lass whose face is brown with the sun when the day is done of revel and romp and race. . . .'

and another:

> 'Somewhere far beyond the
> place where men and women and motors
> race through canyons of the town –
> somewhere on top of the world –
> there is a peak which dull care has
> never climbed.
> You can go there lighthearted in a Jordan
> Playboy – for it's always happy
> in the hills.
> A car for a man's man – that's certain
> Or the girl who loves to take to the open road with top down, in the summer time. . . .'

Jordan, in addition to telling the prospective buyer nothing at all, hedged his bets beautifully, with the same car directed at both men and women – for Ned Jordan knew where the power behind the cheque-book lay. It sold cars by the thousands, and started an entirely new type of communication between seller and customer. We still use it.

Post-war America turned to peacetime production rapidly. An early offering was this 1922 Wills St. Claire, designed by C. H. Wills who had helped in the development of the Model T Ford. It was a finely made V8.

Ford made over 2 million Model T cars in 1923 and by the time the long production run was ended, had made over 15 million. This is a late Model T coupé of 1926.

Ford, who had earlier made a solemn promise to return all profits made on war contracts, had built military vehicles, aircraft engines, and sub-chasing boats, but quickly returned to the marketplace with the Model T in 1919, hitting his first annual million in 1922 and a fantastic two million the following year at his huge superplant, the Rouge, at Dearborn. In this vast complex, blast furnaces turned out the basic metals for most of the cars, and foundries cast 800 cylinder blocks a day, served by 90 miles of railroad track. By the time the Model A was launched in 1927, the Rouge company employed 75,000 men, of which a regiment 5,000 did nothing but clean the place.

Above right: Henry Ford closed down his works for five months in 1927 pending the launching of his new Model A, redesigned to suit the quickening pace of American life. A 65-mph, 200-cu.-in., four-cylinder engine and greatly improved lines were its prime features, and the Model A sold some 5 million before production was brought to an end in 1931.

VINTAGE EUROPE

French gear-maker André Citroën searched around for post-war work for his Paris factory, and by 1919 had made his first small car, one of the first in Europe to be delivered, complete, to customers who previously would have ordered a chassis, then a separate body to their own specifications. Citroën's little Type A was the simplest of machines, with a 1·3-litre side-valve engine. The car, said some critics, 'neither went well nor stopped well', but nonetheless it must have pleased its public as the factory on the Quai Javel was turning them (and the later Type B) out at a rate of 10,000 a year by 1922. Citroën were also making a half-track vehicle based on the 9-hp B2 for military use and for rough terrain; the Kegresse made history in the fashion of the day, when long difficult safaris were considered the most dramatic way of attracting attention to an automotive product, by making two such gruelling treks, one across the Sahara in 1922, followed by a gargantuan 12,500-mile journey across the whole of Africa in 1924–5.

Citroën was always ahead in innovation and promotion, and his line of increasingly popular cars was given an extra boost by his cheap *tout acier* (all steel) cars in 1925 (production 100,000 in 1929). Finally, at the 1934 Paris Salon, he revealed his *pièce de résistance*, the *Traction Avant*, the first practical front-wheel-drive vehicle to be produced in quantity and one that took Europe by storm. Its 1·6-litre 'floating power' four-cylinder engine which drove the front wheels gave it a road-holding character that had never

Above: The Citroën half-track, introduced in 1922 and designed for military use and for rough terrain, achieved fame for its gruelling safari trips in 1922 and 1924.

Above centre: The Citroën Type A of 1919 was the first car to be mass-produced in France. A simple and basic 1·3-litre vehicle, it was well suited to a post-war France eager to buy mobility on a short purse.

before been experienced, and the low-slung car became a motoring milestone.

Meanwhile in Britain young W. O. Bentley had been designing a completely new car (most others in post-war Britain were re-clad 1914 models), a 3-litre sporting vehicle that could cruise at a steady 60 mph all day. Bentley's team worked through the summer of 1919 and managed to get a car into the motor show that year. It took a couple of years before the public was offered the first 3 litre, and at the stiff price of £1,395 it was only for the wealthy sportsman. However, although no other offerings of its type cost within £500 of its price, neither could they match its performance of a power-packed 80 mph on Brooklands banked circuit.

Bentley 3-litre cars secured a place for themselves in a number of major competitions, notably the 1922 Tourist Trophy, and a string of victories at Le Mans. Altogether just 1,630 3-litre cars were produced between 1921 and 2929 and a good many of them have survived to become treasures that can today command the price of a family-sized house. 'W.O.' made his 3-litre car in short- and long-chassis form (Red and Blue Labels) and in 1926 attempted to attract the carriage trade with a somewhat unsuccessful 6·5 litre. Undaunted, Bentley developed this into his legendary 200 bhp Speed 6 which won the last two 'Bentley Le Mans'.

Down-market England was alive to the brief post-war boom before the first depression hit in 1921. William Morris had started in 1913 with his 1018-cc Oxford. He had been producing 100 a month by the beginning of the 1914 war and had started to offer the larger Cowley (the Oxford had only two seats to the Cowley's two or four) which housed an American Continental Red Seal unit of 1·5 litres snapped up by Morris at an astonishing price of just over £25 each, including gearbox. When U-Boats sent half of them to the bottom of the Atlantic it caused merely a hiccup in production.

When the market dropped in the spring of 1921, Morris, who had quickly re-aligned the civilian markets, slashed £100 off his £525 Cowley and cut the Oxford by £90 after observing Henry Ford do the same, forcing his British competitors to copy him. Young William – he still was only 28 – not

Right: The 'Bullnose' Morris Oxford of 1922. William Morris doubled his output this year after slashing prices the previous spring – and trebled it in 1923. The basic design dates from 1911.

Britain's Austin Seven appeared in 1922 to press comments of the 'Get one for each foot' type, but Herbert Austin's baby-car design was right on target and his car gave wheels to more family motorists than any other British car of the time. This is a Seven saloon of about 1928.

Top right: Developed from engineer Laurence Pomeroy's Prince Henry Vauxhall (so named after its participation in the 1910 Prince Henry Trials in Germany), the 4·5-litre 30/98 Vauxhall was first made in 1913 but had to wait until 1919 for its emergence as the fast tourer that sold to both family and sporting motorists.

Right: One of the most respected British marques of vintage days, the Coventry-made Alvis was built on principles of quality and performance. Modest of thirst and sporting at speed, this robust 1927 12/50 sports tourer had hard-living, unburstable qualities that endeared it to all.

only increased his profit, but doubled his output in 1922, trebled it the next year, and doubled it again in 1923! His sales broke the Ford Model T monopoly in Britain, although his main competitor, Clyno, was, by this time, making cars (using a Coventry-Climax engine of 1366 cc that had the edge in quality on the Morris product) which were selling for the same price. Clyno, sadly, cut its costs too much in 1929, offering a '£100 car', and the resultant loss broke the Staffordshire company.

Herbert Austin had a vigour similar to Morris, although their temperaments were quite different. Herbert had, by 1922, introduced the first of his light cars. Considerably lighter and smaller than the Morris Cowley, Austin's 'mini' was eventually to set the trend of small-car philosophy that even influences today's designers. The diminutive Austin Seven rapidly became a trendsetter for the mass-market. It was right on the button! It was the right size for the new public, it looked enough like a real motor car to allay any qualms about buying some cardboard-and-string cyclecar; and it was, above all, the right price (£225 in 1922), particularly now that the U.S.A. had shown the way to that slightly-wicked-but-wonderful way of delaying financial nemesis – the hire-purchase system.

Austin had introduced his 'Heavy 12' in 1921 just before the Seven, which completely overshadowed it. However, the survival of the company owed as much to the plain-Jane-Twelve, sometimes hailed as the 'hardest-wearing car of all time' as it did to the smaller model. It was one of Austin's most successful designs and was almost indestructible. Gleaming examples are still seen today changing hands at auctions held in various parts of Europe.

In the sportscar field, Vauxhall was making history with its 30/98, developed from the famed pre-war Prince Henry, winning countless hill climbs, trials and races. Aston Martin – prototype seen first in 1919 – was providing strong sporting competition, but was to go through some trauma before being re-designed in 1926 as an overhead-camshaft 1·5-litre. Another Coventry-based company, Alvis, was making a sporty little car on the principles of long life, high quality and interesting performance, and Alvis was to become one of the best-favoured marques of British vintage days. Cecil Kimber of Morris Garages was engaged in 1923 in modifying one of his Morris products into another much-loved sports vehicle, the MG.

The respected Rover company was also scanning the market for quantity outlets, and had come up with a small car, the Rover 8, as early as 1905. Now it offered a rugged but somewhat 'Mickey Mouse' two-seater 8 with a small flat-twin air-cooled unit that stuck out of the sides of the bonnet like little ears. They were cowled, it was said, to prevent nervous passengers from leaping out of the car when the finned cylinders became red-hot with over-exercise.

Germany was also casting round the 'marginal motorist' market. Opel had produced the *Puppchen*, a feminine little four-seater, just before the war. Now in the Twenties the firm needed a mass-made car for the German public who were struggling back to solvency after the horrors of the runaway inflation of 1923 (Opel had on occasions been forced to print its own money to pay its employees at Russelsheim!).

The little Citroën 5CV of 1922 inspired the German firm to produce a similar car (it proved too similar, and became the cause of a lawsuit) which helped revive the company's and the country's financial climate in no small way. The Opel 4/12 was dubbed *Laubfrosch* (Tree frog), largely because of its revolting green paintwork. The first assembly-line-produced Laubfrosch boat-tailed two-seaters had a simple 951-cc side-valve unit with a two-bearing crankshaft and gravity feed tank. This and later versions sold like hot *Pfannkuchen* and some 65,000 of them turned Germany's roads green for the next five years.

The French Peugeot company had also joined the small-car game as had Italy with its Fiat 1·5-litre 501, although that company still tended to make larger-engined cars of up to 4·7 litres during this period, probably as there was no strong mass market in Italy. Fiat came into line in 1925, however, with the 990-cc 509, the first genuine quantity-produced vehicle the country had made.

The Rover with the Mickey Mouse ears (discreetly hidden here) was launched in 1920. Designed by J. Y. Sangster of later motor-cycle fame, its flat-twin air-cooled unit stuck out into the air each side of the bonnet—or hood—but still heated up to dull red under stress. Its original 1-litre engine was later enlarged to 1300 cc.

Right: The 951-cc 12-hp Laubfrosch, or Tree Frog, produced by Opel in 1924, gave the company a strong shot in the arm at a time when the German economy was struggling back to solvency and stability.

One of the super-powerful line of Mercedes-Benz sports vehicles of the late Twenties, the 1927 S, with a six-cylinder 6·79-litre super-charged engine.

During the decade, economic boom followed by depression and then recovery influenced automotive production not only in quantity but in size and quality. Those with faith in the crests of commerce put their money into up-market transport in addition to bread-and-butter investment. Daimler, maker of the powerful Mercedes range (not officially amalgamated with Benz until 1926), showed its faith in its own products by producing, in 1922, a range of powerful blown 4- and 6-litre cars. By 1926, with Ferdinand Porsche in charge of the design office, Daimler-Benz, while making solid vehicles like the Stuttgart and the Nurburg in saloon form, was on the threshold of creating its highly sportive touring car, the model K, with a 6·5-litre supercharged engine. This, in turn, was developed into the stunningly powerful S, the later SS and its short-chassis partner the SSK, a two-seater so-called tourer which was fast enough to win races against the best the rest of the world could put on the starting grid.

For the more cautious European motorists with a large purse, there was the Grosser Mercedes (1930), the most luxurious of them all, favoured during the following years by Nazi party chiefs for its impressive bulk and style.

French *automobilistes* were always strongly nationalistic about anything they bought and used, and the élite of the day would purr silently about in their 45-hp Renault or Hispano-Suiza torpedoes. Belgians of rank travelled in their dignified straight-eight Minerva from Antwerp, Italians slid smoothly over the Appenines in the Milan-made Isotta-Franschini, and the Dutch toured the tulip fields in the finely engineered Spyker.

Britain had its never-to-be-spoken-of-in-the-same-breath-as-any-other-car Rolls-Royce Silver Ghost, which, by 1925, was about to retire in favour of the smart Phantom I. There was, too, the English Daimler, still the favourites of the Royal Family; the big Leyland Eight tourer; and, of a somewhat more dashing genre, the Alvis and the London-region based Lagonda, the car that had grown up from a cycle-type tri-car made by Ohio-born Wilbur Gunn in 1905 to blossom as a superbly finished sports-tourer by the mid-Twenties.

The United States also has its élite: Packard, Peerless and Pierce-Arrow, the quality trio; Duesenberg, Cadillac and Rolls-Royce Phantom I made in Springfield, Massachusetts, from 1927 to 1932. The last of the raccoon-coat roadsters were still around but the Mercer, once a stripped-down sporting bucket, had become too staid and was to die in 1925. The old spartan Stutz Bearcat Speedster, once the joy of the boys in the straw hats and blazers, had now developed into what was called the 'Safety Stutz', but its speedster option, the Black Hawk, which was placed second at Le Mans in 1928, could show a dusty rear end to any U.S. automobile except the vaunted Duesenberg.

The Twenties saw both the birth of the small quantity-made car for the man in the street, and the emergence of the great dream cars – the sort of bullet-bonneted sportscar with a cocktail cabinet in every door recess, a car in which you raced the Blue Train down to the French Riviera. Dreams were as near as most ever came to owning one, but they lent colour to a grey period of post-war recovery. Most of the world's populace had to wait a decade, until the Thirties, to possess a genuine shiny motor car and often found that, by then, the shine was the best part of the product.

By the end of the Twenties it was obvious that motor manufacturing was changing its entire approach. Small firms were on the way out. Ten years earlier about 80 companies in Britain had produced 25,000 cars. In 1929 half the number of car makers built nearly 250,000 vehicles. By that year there were 260,000 registered vehicles on the roads of Britain (all restricted still to the 1903 Act which limited speeds to 20 mph), and mass-produced cars were beginning to herald the age of the first traffic jams.

Far left: A Rolls-Royce from Springfield, Massachusetts, U.S.A. This Brewster-bodied Phantom I of 1927 was one of 1,241 examples made in the American works from 1927 to 1931.

Below: One of the more modest power units of the late Twenties, the engine of a Fiat 525S of 1929. It has six cylinders, 3739 cc and 65·8 bhp at 3200 rpm.

Bottom: From 1900 to 1937 Auburn, Indiana, was the home of one of the most distinguished American luxury sporting vehicles, the Auburn. Redesigned in 1924, the Auburn was considered the smartest car made in the U.S.A. This is the classic straight-eight Boat-tailed Speedster 120.

Post-Vintage Thoroughbreds

If the Twenties had been a decade of hugely increasing numbers, of great changes in design and in construction methods, the Thirties were to be times of a geometric increase on the roads and a reduction in overall quality. Small underpowered cars made for small under-financed family owners. The vintage days of the automobile were over.

There were, however, exceptions to the normal run-of-the-mill car. Some of the most elegant and powerful, if not the most logically engineered vehicles, were made during the Thirties, cars whose images of romance and luxurious living, of the sporting life with a scarf flowing in the wind are still with many of us even today. Here in the following pages are just a handful of these cars, now rightfully included with the products of the halcyon days of motoring – the post-vintage thoroughbreds.

An end-of-vintage Bugatti. This Type 49, made in 1931, has a bizarre history. Owned by an Irish woman living in France, it was dismantled and hidden by her chauffeur in 1940 to avoid confiscation by invading Nazi forces. Unfortunately the chauffeur was killed during the war, and the car remained hidden until 1973, when it was re-assembled. The engine is a straight-eight with 3257-cc capacity and a single overhead camshaft.

Above: Citroën gained popularity with the launch of the 'Traction Avant', the car all Europe was waiting for in 1934. Its stability and roadholding qualities were truly phenomenal for the day, and the 7CV, with its 'floating-power' engine and advance styling, coupled with the then revolutionary front-wheel drive, created a high demand for this French car.

Left: A rare post-vintage thoroughbred of which, it is said, there are only two survivors – the 1934 Aston Martin Mk II Le Mans two-seater sports model. Developed from the team of cars that won its class in the 1931 Le Mans 24 Hours Race and others that year, the Le Mans model was an immediate success. The engine is a four-cylinder, 1493-cc, single ohc.

Right: If not quite out of the thoroughbred stable, this little 1934 Morgan Aero gave more pleasure to the run-of-the-mill young enthusiasts than many other more aristocratic marques. For those who had a deep longing to get behind the wheel of a sports car this was (almost) the answer. Powered by its exposed V-twin JAP 1096-cc unit, it must have had the handling characteristics of a light aircraft!

Above: The inescapable Bentley. This 4·5-litre Airline Saloon, a thoroughbred in all its aspects, was run in open form until 1936 when its owner had this saloon body fitted. One can see the beginning of the development of the elegant post-war Mulliner fastback Bentley Continental in its racy lines.

Left: The word Jaguar was first seen on the products of William Lyons's SS Car Company of Coventry in 1936 when they were called Jaguar-SS. But when SS became more likely to stand for *Schutzstaffel*, Jaguar was used alone, and in 1945 the company changed its name to Jaguar Cars Limited. This is the smart 1608-cc saloon of 1937.